A Horseman's Handbook

Basic Riding Explained

Georgie Henschel

Ward Lock Limited · London

Acknowledgments

In gratitude to all: teachers, friends, pupils and horses, without whose help throughout the years I would not have been able to write this book. Special thanks to Leslie Lane for the photographs; to the riders, young and older, who appear in the illustrations; and to Alison Oliver and Sue Allfrey for kindly letting us use their amenities.

Georgie Henschel

The publishers are grateful to Alison Sherred for the USA emendations.

Previous page Out for a ride on a sunny morning. A hard hat must always be worn, even when riding gently.
Opposite Correct and comfortable clothes for learning to ride: hard hat, jodhpurs and jodhpur boots. Riding without stirrups improves the position.

© Georgie Henschel 1980

First published in Great Britain in 1980
by Ward Lock Limited, 116 Baker Street,
London W1M 2BB, a Pentos Company

All Rights Reserved. No part of this publication may be reproduced, stored in a retrieval system, or transmitted, in any form or by any means, electronic, mechanical, photocopying, recording, or otherwise, without the prior permission of the Copyright owner.

House editor Suzanna Osman Jones

Text set in Times

Printed and bound in Great Britain by
Clark-Constable Ltd, Edinburgh

British Library Cataloguing in Publication Data

Henschel, Georgie
Basic riding explained. — (Horseman's handbooks). —
  (Concorde books).
  1. Horsemanship
  I. Title   II. Series   III. Series
  798'.23   SF309
  ISBN 0-7063-5958-5
  ISBN 0-7063-5959-3 Pbk

Contents

1 Riding in today's world   4
2 Communicating with the horse   10
3 Riding the gaits   19
4 Balance and co-ordination   42
5 Enjoy your riding   49
6 Choosing and caring for a horse   65
7 The mind of the horse   91
   Glossary of US equivalents   96
   Useful addresses   96

1 Riding in today's world

Riding today, and show jumping in particular, has, at its top competitive level, become one of the world's most popular spectator sports. Internationally successful riders, and their mounts, enjoy the same kind of recognition, and adulation which earlier this century was enjoyed by male and female film stars.

Perhaps it is this which has put riding itself into a somewhat false perspective. Even among the many thousands of riders who will never become 'stars', the slant seems to be more and more towards competitive achievement, and away from riding for pleasure; this is a pity, because riding is not only one of the most truly recreative and pleasurable occupations left to us in this mechanical age, but also one of the most healthy.

This accent on competitive riding is something fairly new. It's not so very long ago that more or less everyone rode; not because it was 'the thing to do', but because it was necessary. Not that everyone rode specially well, or could have passed their Pony Club or their Riding Club grade tests. But until the motor car became universal, it was taken for granted that unless people were senile or physically incapacitated, they were all capable of riding to wherever they wanted to go.

That riding was a healthy way of getting about is abundantly proved by our ancestors, the majority of whom, in all layers of society, ate far heavier meals than we do today, and mostly drank far more with those meals. They would probably all have succumbed to over-indulgence at an early age if they hadn't been able to shake up their livers by riding to and from their meetings, dinners, fairs, and general get-togethers. 'The best thing for the inside of a man is the outside of a horse' was a true saying for them. It is just as true for us today, for although we may eat, and possibly drink, less than they did, we take on the whole far less exercise and have more worries and mental stresses. Learn to ride, and the pleasure of doing something in the company of another living creature, combined with concentrating on the skills necessary to stay on its back, and worries and mental stresses will, for the time being, disappear. Physical stresses you will have at first, but those will be overcome. And anyway, to be tired physically is a good thing; the body's need for rest subdues the too-active mind.

What makes riding unique among sports it that it is the only one which not only involves learning how to do it, but how to obtain the confidence and co-operation of one's horse. Learning to play golf or tennis, for example, we can lose our tempers: we can even break our clubs or our rackets with no damage except to our purses. We cannot behave similarly when learning to ride. All the time we are trying to do the right things with our bodies, we have to remember we are sitting on a living animal whose willing co-operation is necessary to our progress. We must control our minds and tempers as well as our bodies. Riding is also unique, in that once we have become reasonably competent, it enables us to go out and enjoy the sights and sounds of the countryside, of which we will see far more from our horses than from our cars, or even from our own feet. Birds and wild animals are not nearly so shy if we are mounted. The horse to them is another animal, the person on its back, a part of it, and therefore not frightening. Nor is there any need to ride in a group, or even with one companion, to enjoy the countryside. Our horse is our companion, and like our dog, will become more companionable the more thought and care we give to it, and to the way we ride it.

By and large, there is no better recreation than riding for twentieth century — and probably twenty-first century — man, woman or child, provided it is undertaken in the spirit of something to be enjoyed for its own sake, and done as well as each person's ability allows. If you turn out to be a 'natural', with the talent to become a brilliant rider, so much the better; but it should always be riding itself which gives you pleasure; not riding in order to win competitions on horseback.

Another advantage of riding over most other sports is that one can ride, and ride well, into old age. At what other sport could a lady of seventy, Mrs Lorna Johnstone, have represented her country with distinction at the Olympics? Nor, contrary to popular belief, is one ever too old to learn, provided one limits one's ambition to becoming competent enough to enjoy oneself on a reliable horse. Learn to ride in your fifties, even your sixties if you like, and you will enjoy a healthy and active old age. Riding keeps the body supple, unstiffens those joints that tend to stiffen with the years, and because no two rides are ever the same, keeps the mind alert and continually looking forward. It is when we stop looking forward with enjoyment that we begin to feel old.

Children on the other hand can start too young, unless they are very keen. Children are often pushed into riding because their parents think they ought to. Never force a child to ride, or make it continue if it wants to stop for some reason that may seem to you silly or inadequate. Children, above all, should get pleasure from riding, and from their ponies. It is a mistake for parents to try to satisfy their ambitions vicariously by forcing their children into the competitive rat-race on expensive ponies when most of them would probably far rather be playing cowboys and Indians on unfashionable nondescripts. Anyone teaching young children should remember that however keen they may be, they can only concentrate for short periods at a time.

For centuries, riding was to a vast number of people as natural and necessary a part of life as eating or sleeping. It is part of a great many people's lives today, although no longer a necessity. Or perhaps it is. If we are to survive as a species and not turn into a vast conglomerate of automatons, surely it is necessary that we keep some contact with the natural world around us and other of its inhabitants. Many must realize this, consciously or unconsciously; which is perhaps why there are today so many hippophiles; so many who, if they can't already do so, want desperately to learn to ride.

A good position preparatory to coming downhill. The pony is on a good contact, the rider's legs are close to its sides and her back is nicely straight, her shoulders wide and free. She is well prepared to hold an even pace down the hill.

The principles of riding

Riding is an art. Don't let that discourage you. Music, painting, literature, dancing, and so on, are all arts, yet many people who will never be artists themselves get a lot of pleasure from practising them, because they have taken the trouble to learn their basic principles, or techniques, and to become competent.

Before you get on a horse, therefore, it is worth considering the basic principles, or techniques, of riding. It will help you to understand the various things your instructor, or books on riding, will tell you to do when on a horse.

The first principle of riding is that it is primarily a matter of *balance*. Horses are not born with riders on their backs. A young horse has to learn how to carry, or balance, a rider. The better a rider's balance is in accord with the horse's movement, the better the horse will go, and the more comfortably the rider will ride.

Because balance is so important, it follows that *relaxation* is almost equally so. Any sport or activity requiring balance calls for a relaxed co-ordination of joints and muscles. If you remember learning to ride a bicycle, you will remember that the harder you tried to hold the thing up, and yourself on it, the more often it fell down and you fell off. Only when you stopped trying so hard and 'went with' the movement of the wheels, did you succeed. A horse is far easier to sit on than a bicycle. Because it has four legs, it will not fall down if you lose your balance, it is only you who will probably hit the ground. The majority of falls are caused by loss of balance, not lack of grip. It is important to remember this.

To be balanced, relaxed and co-ordinated on a horse, it helps to think of *rhythm*. A horse, in each of its gaits, moves in a distinct rhythm which it is up to you to feel, to accept, and to go with, in balance.

The rhythm of a particular gait is the beat of the strides. The beat of the walk is *four*, because each leg is coming to the ground separately, and should do so in absolutely true rhythm.

The beat of the trot is *two*, because the legs come to the ground in pairs, diagonally.

The beat of the canter is *three*, and the footfall is rather more complicated. If a horse is cantering on a circle to the right, and is therefore 'leading' with the off-foreleg, the footfall, or leg sequence, will be: near-hind, off-hind and near-fore diagonally together, then off-fore, followed by a moment of suspension when all four legs are off the ground. If it is circling to the left, the near-foreleg leading, the leg sequence will be reversed.

'Off' means right-hand side; 'near' means left-hand side.

In the gallop, the fastest pace, when the horse is stretched out to its full length, the beat is *four*, because the two legs which in canter come to the ground diagonally together, now come down separately — the leg sequence, off-foreleg leading, being: near-hind, off-hind, near-fore, off-fore; suspension.

Watch horses moving at different paces, either live, or on television, and you will see these beats and footfalls for yourself. Then watch the riders. The good ones will appear to be 'part of' their horses, not only because they are sitting correctly and are in balance, but because they are in rhythm with them.

As your riding progresses, there will be occasions when you will need to use grip, but balance will always be more important.

You do not need physical strength to ride, or to control a horse. The term 'a strong rider' doesn't mean the rider is the equivalent of a muscle-bound weight-lifter. It means that the rider knows exactly how to communicate his, or her, wishes to the horse, and has the experience, the confidence and the mental dominance to insist that those wishes are obeyed, even by the recalcitrant or the delinquent! Once you learn the correct ways of communicating your wishes to your horse, *tact* and *accuracy* are far more important than strength. After all, even the smallest Shetland pony is stronger than most humans.

Don't think you have to be particularly bold or daring to learn to ride. Many people get a lot of pleasure from riding without feeling they have to jump enormous obstacles, or gallop flat out across country. You can ride according to your temperament and your desires; if you are nervous at first, do not be ashamed of admitting it. Remember, if you are taking lessons, that a good instructor will never mount you on a horse which is beyond your ability to manage. As your ability develops, so will your courage, and your confidence.

Confidence can only come with experience; and through never, at any stage, trying to do what you know is beyond your ability. Nevertheless, it is the supreme achievement, and should never be confused with the foolhardiness of the novice, who, wanting to appear brave, will 'have a go', probably disastrously, at anything!

2 Communicating with the horse

The aids

The rider communicates his wishes to the horse by means of what are called 'the aids'. These 'aids' are really a code of signals which all horses that have been competently broken and schooled have been taught to understand. When you are learning to ride, therefore, and your horse either does not do what you want, or does something quite different, you may be pretty sure it is you who have given it the wrong signals, or 'aids'.

The natural aids are: *seat*, *legs*, *hands* and *voice*.

The seat is obviously what you sit on. What is not so obvious is how it can affect and influence the horse. A good way to discover this is to sit on a hard chair with your hand underneath you. If you are sitting upright, head up and shoulders squared, there will be considerable pressure on your hand. If you round your shoulders, poke your head forward and sit on your fork rather than your seat bones, there will be little pressure on your hand. Sit upright again, and turn your body right, or left, and you will feel more pressure on one seat bone than the other. Now, sit down very deeply as though you were trying to push the chair through the floor, and your hand will feel squashed.

The horse feels all these different pressures, and responds to them. The extra firm downward pressure will tell it you want it to go forward; the lateral pressure on the seat bones, which will occur naturally when you are bending your horse to right or left, will help it to do so correctly; the ordinary sitting-on-hand pressure should be the normal contact of your seat with the saddle. Poke your head forward, round your shoulders and sit on your fork, and your seat will have lost most of its power of influence.

Above ... and there you are. Here, the rider is in the correct position: head up, straight line from shoulders down to seat, back neither stiff, nor hollowed; supple knee and ankle, the heel coming under the seat, the stirrup held on the ball of the foot. The hands rounded, thumbs uppermost, the reins carried just in front of the saddle. As well as looking comfortable, the rider is in a position of balance, ready to take up, and 'go with' the forward movement of the horse.

Above right Here, the rider shows what not to do: sit on your fork, stiffen and hollow the small of your back, tip your lower leg back. You can see that already, even at halt, the rider looks off balance, and is finding it necessary to bring the hands back as the body tips forward.

The seat, however, does not work entirely on is own; it works in conjunction with the *legs*. The part of the leg which is used as an aid is the inside of the calf, in riding parlance called the 'lower leg'. For the lower leg to be effective as an aid, it is important not to turn the points of the knees inwards as though trying to hold the saddle in a vice-like grip between them. If the thighs are laid against the saddle, not clenched on to it, and the knee joints left supple, the lower leg will naturally hang straight down from the knee, the inside calf against the horse's side.

Here, the rider is 'behind the movement'; seat right to the back of the saddle, lower leg stuck forward. Although he looks more comfortable than in the last picture, he would find it impossible to stand in his stirrups without adjusting his leg position, and impossible to rise to the trot correctly; moreover, his lower leg, stuck forward and away from the horse's side, is not doing its job as an 'aid'. From the horse's point of view the rider's weight is uncomfortably far back.

To understand why the seat and the legs should work in conjunction, one must understand that the horse works from behind: it impels itself forward from the hindquarters. Downward pressure of the seat combined with inward pressure of the lower leg sets the horse in motion: starts the engine, as it were. Raising the seat in an uphill bicycling movement will not set the horse going; nor will sitting on your fork, banging away with your heels, or throwing the reins at it.

The seat and the legs ask for, and produce, forward movement. The *hands* control the speed of the movement, and help to indicate its direction. Because the hands connect through the reins with the bit in the horse's mouth, it is fairly obvious that they should be both sensitive and sympathetic. This will not be possible until your seat — that basic part of you which is attached to the saddle — can stay attached without the necessity of holding on to anything. To have good hands is every horseman's ambition; these are entirely dependent on having a good, firm and independent seat.

Voice is more important than is often realized. Horses have a very acute sense of hearing and are quick to recognize and respond to different tones of voice. A calm, soothing voice will often help to settle an excitable horse, particularly if the same word is always used: 'gently' . . . or 'quietly', or whatever comes to your mind. It is not a good plan to use the voice, or constant clicking noises, to urge a horse on. When riding in company this can result in making other peoples' horses respond rather than one's own. A cross voice, 'NO', said very firmly, will often make a horse think twice about shying, or doing whatever other silly thing he may have contemplated. You should never shout at your horse. The shout sounds far louder to him than it does to you. Shouting at a horse going in to a jump is far more likely to distract its attention than encourage it to perform.

There is one other natural aid which is hardly ever mentioned, but which nevertheless exists; that is *mental* aid. This is not inferring that there is some sort of ESP between horse and rider, although undoubtedly a horse that is constantly ridden by the same rider will often appear to be obeying the rider's thoughts rather than his actual aids. Mental aid really means thinking about the aids you are going to give the horse fractionally before you do so: preparing him for them. For instance, if you and your horse have been standing relaxed, looking at the view or listening to your instructor, think about moving off before you do so; this will bring your body back into attention, the horse will sense that you are going to ask for something, and be ready to walk forward briskly. If you just sit there limply, then gather up the reins like yards of knitting and dig the horse in the ribs, you will surprise it out of its inattention, it will trip over its feet in its hurry to do something and your instructor will probably shout at you! Mental aid also means a little more; it means being certain in your own mind of what your are going to ask the horse to do, and equally certain that you can make him do it. Horses are large, strong animals. In the end, however well we ride and accurately we use all the aids, it is with our minds, not our physical strength, that we control them and obtain their willing obedience.

Mounting

It is now time to get on to a horse, and put into practice some of the aids we have been discussing.

Before mounting, check the length of the stirrup by holding it out under your arm; your fingers at the stirrup bar, the flat of the iron in your armpit. This may not be quite accurate, as some people have short arms and long legs, and some, vice versa, but it is a good guide. Now, stand beside the horse, your left shoulder to his left shoulder, and pick up the reins. Take the buckle in your right hand, then take both reins together in your left, about a third of the way up, the outside one a little shorter than the inside. Remove your right hand from the buckle, and now put your left foot in the stirrup. (If your jodhpurs, breeches or jeans are very tight, you may find this difficult!) Now, put your left hand, holding the reins, on the horse's withers, your right hand across the pommel of the saddle, push yourself up on to your left foot, without sticking your toe into the horse's side, swing your right leg over the horse's quarters, and lower yourself on to the saddle. The first time you do this, you will probably land with a bump; never mind, the first horse you mount will be used to beginners and will probably not object, and anyway, you will try to do better next time. Once arrived on top, don't let go of the reins. Sit yourself comfortably in the middle, the deepest part of the saddle, and put your right foot in the stirrup. Now is the time to check your stirrups for length. To do this, take your feet out again, and let your legs hang down. The correct length for ordinary riding, if you have normal legs, is when the bottom of the iron reaches to, or to JUST below, your ankle bone. As the proper way to alter the length of your stirrups when mounted is to keep your feet in the stirrups while doing so, you may as well learn how to do this right away. Put your feet back into them, and keep hold of the reins, in the left hand when adjusting the right stirrup, and vice versa. Now, take your weight off your foot, take hold of the leather below the buckle, and pull the buckle downwards. Then, with your thumb on top of the leather, slip the tongue of

left hand on withers, left foot in stirrup . . .

. . . spring up . . .

. right leg over the back .

Shortening the stirrups without taking the foot out. The saddle here has a 'half-cut-back' head (pommel); the numnah is well put on, not pressing on the withers, and you can see how it is held in place, the strap coming over the front of the saddle and slipping through one of the girth straps. The girth is nylon, and the young rider is wearing jodhpurs and jodhpur boots; a much more suitable, comfortable, and correct get-up for the young than the ubiquitous rubber riding boots.

the buckle out of its hole, and guide it up, or down, the necessary number of holes. Then pull down on the back of the leather until the buckle is up to the bar again. Change hands, and repeat on the other side. Put the stirrup under the ball of your foot, that is, under your big toe joint. This is one part of one's foot that has some feeling; one can actually wriggle one's big toe joint, and so really feel the stirrup under it. There is a correct way of putting the foot into the stirrup; that is, with the front of the stirrup turned outwards. There is a reason for this apparently pernickety detail. Should you fall off, the stirrup will turn back openly towards the saddle and allow your foot to free itself. If your foot is in the wrong way round, with the back of the stirrup outwards, the stirrup will fall back inwards, and could trap your foot between itself and the horse.

Now, having sorted out the stirrups, pick up the reins. The extraordinary thing about reins is that people who can pick up and carry things with their hands in perfectly normal positions, will do the oddest things with those same hands when on a horse. In fact, the hand position is precisely that of picking up, and carrying two small objects. It helps to think that you are

Tightening the girth when mounted. This is a lampwick girth; tubular, and with two buckles. This picture shows very clearly the saddle's continental panel, and lets you see how closely the leg can lie against the horse's side, when the saddle panel is not padded. Here, the strap around the horse's neck is part of a running martingale; if it were a neckstrap, you can see how useful it might be to the novice rider in an emergency.

carrying your reins, rather than *holding* them. The carrying position is quite different from the holding one. Try it out and see. Pick up two small glasses of water and carry them about, not spilling them. Your hands will be rounded, thumbs uppermost, there will be a straight line from them to your elbows, which will be bent and supple, and there will be more or less a right angle between your upper and lower arms. Now, hold on to a bar, or the back of a chair, and your hands will be turned, backs uppermost, your arms straight, and your elbows fixed. If when riding you have trouble with your hand position, practise this carrying exercise.

The reins should be carried just in front of the saddle, a little above it, the hands about the same distance apart as the width of a bit in the horse's mouth. If, when you have the reins in your hands, you can imagine those two glasses of water, you will automatically make two rounded fists, which can loosen or tighten their feel of the reins by a movement of the fingers. It will also help you to keep the line: elbow, wrist, horse's mouth, and to keep your wrists soft.

A word about elbows: while the old saying that you should keep them close to your sides is correct, it does not mean that you should keep them fixed to your sides, as though there were adhesive between them and your jacket; it simply means that they should not stick out *sideways*. In fact, your elbows should never feel fixed, or locked, in position. They must be able to move forwards or backwards, straight; a movement similar to that of a piston.

You are now sitting on your horse. Your head is up, your shoulders squared, your seat is in the middle of the saddle, your thighs laid against it, your knees supple, your lower leg straight down, just feeling the horse's sides, your stirrups under the ball of your foot, your ankle supple so that your toe is just higher than your heel. You have picked up the reins and are carrying them in two rounded unclenched fists; all comfortable and correct. Before you go forward into walk, you had better discover how to get off the horse.

Take the reins in your left hand; take both feet out of the stirrups. Turn your body slightly to the right. Put your right hand on the pommel in front of you, swing your right leg over the horse's quarters and drop lightly to the ground. In your relief at finding yourself there, *don't drop the reins!* The routine, when dismounted, and the horse is to be led, is this. Take the reins over the horse's head and slip your left arm through them, so that you have both hands free. Run up the stirrups. That is: slide the iron up the underside of the leather, then run the leather through the iron so that it doesn't slip down. Go round the front of the horse and repeat on the off side. Come back; slacken your girth a couple of holes. Keeping your left arm through the reins, take them together in your right hand, about a foot from the bit, and walk on. Never let the end of the reins trail on the ground; sooner or later you or the horse will tread on them if you do.

Having discovered how to mount, and dismount, you are now ready to go forward into walk.

3 Riding the gaits

The walk

The moment a horse moves into walk, you should be conscious of the four regular beats of its legs. The very first time a horse walks forward under you, trying to feel this beat will help you not to stiffen up with anxiety. Sit up straight, sit on all your seat, not only on your seat bones, but don't tense the muscles of your buttocks. Sit deep and softly, your loins relaxed so that your hip joints can follow, or give to, the movement of the horse. Don't tense your thighs; let your knees and ankles be supple, and your lower leg will lie close to the horse's sides and be able to feel the slight movement of its barrel.

To feel, and go with, the rhythm of walk, it helps to imagine that from the waist down, you have grown four legs. It also helps to try to count the beat out loud to yourself . . one, two, three, four. . . You may find at first that you are only counting one . . two . . rather slowly; you are only counting, and feeling what the *forelegs* are doing! Relax your seat. Try to feel what's going on *behind* the saddle. Once your body has found the beat of all four legs, you will discover that without your doing anything else, your horse has begun to walk better. Now, consider your hands.

At the walk, the horse makes a small movement of the head at each stride, it 'nods' its head. Your hands, therefore, must follow this nod, but quietly, almost imperceptibly. Do not push the reins backwards and forwards. Take a light, even feel of the horse's mouth, carry your hands lightly and still, and you will feel the horse move them fractionally as it strides. When you want to halt from walk, you 'stop the nod'. That is, you close and tighten your fist, which also tightens the muscle of your forearm, you close both legs against the horse's sides, sit down

Walking on ... the horse has approached and is passing the camera on a slight left bend, on light contact.

firmly in the saddle, and say 'no' mentally to forward movement. Do not lean back and *pull* on the reins. All riding is forward movement. The halt is forward movement checked, not pulled backwards.

To walk forward from halt, you should first close the fists slightly, so that the horse knows you are going to ask something of it. Then, simultaneously, press downwards with your seat and ask for forward movement with a firm inward squeeze of both legs. If necessary, if the horse does not respond at once, apply a second, firmer squeeze, using your heels. Do *not* take your seat out of the saddle. The moment the horse walks, give to the 'nod'.

It may encourage you to know that many very competent riders do not get their horses walking really well. Sometimes this is because they are concentrating so hard they have forgotten to think of rhythm; more often it is because they are forcing, or hurrying, the walk. That is, asking the horse to walk out of the natural rhythm of its stride.

Every horse, like every human, has its own natural rhythm of stride. One can improve the way a horse uses itself at walk, and there are different degrees of walk, but all should be developed from the horse's natural stride rhythm. Hurrying the horse into an unnatural one will upset the rhythm and quality of all its gaits. If this sounds complicated, let's put it this way. If you feel your horse dawdling along under you, don't just dot him one and ask him to go faster. Take up more contact, to get his attention, then, sitting up straight, put some pressure on your seat, and with seat and legs, ask him to use his back end, to get his quarters under him — to put the engine in gear, as it were. The result will be a walk in the same rhythm, but because the hindquarters are doing some work, a walk with more power: more 'push', or impulsion, from behind.

The different kinds of walk
The free walk is when the horse is striding out naturally, head and neck stretched on to light contact on a long rein. To do this well you must still 'go with' the horse; relaxed, but keeping your body in rhythm with his, allowing him neither to increase nor decrease his speed.

In the medium, which is really the normal or usual walk, the hindquarters are more engaged and the head therefore higher, and the horse in contact with the rider's hand. The stride will be shorter but more energetic than in the free walk.

The collected walk is an advanced gait, when the quarters are fully engaged and lowered, the forehand light, the poll flexed and the horse going forward with great impulsion and strong rhythmic strides into the rider's hand.

When you have developed enough balance, relaxation, and feel for rhythm to produce good free and medium walks from any horse you ride, you are well on your way up the ladder of achievement.

Jogging is an irritating gait that is often caused by the rider being tense and having no idea of rhythm; also by the rider asking the horse to go forward with legs and seat (sometimes by mistake) and then stopping it by hanging on to the reins. If a horse jogs with you, don't tense up and grab the reins. Relax yourself; sit deep into the saddle, think of rhythm. If your seat is deep, and yet soft, and your lower legs close to the horse, you should be able to feel when the walk is about to turn into a jog, and hold the walk rhythm before the horse breaks it. Use your voice.

The trot

To many, the trot seems at first to be a highly uncomfortable, bumpy movement, usually because, being a faster pace, they have tensed themselves against it, hoping to stay aboard by grip instead of balance. When you start riding, you will not know how to 'rise' to the trot, so your first trots will all be, hopefully, 'sitting'. That is, your seat will be expected to remain in the saddle while the horse bounces along, apparently doing its best to jolt you out of whatever balance you had managed to achieve at walk.

Don't despair. You are only uncomfortable because you have tightened all your muscles, hunched your shoulders, drawn up your thighs and legs, turned your toes out and tried to make your legs cling on to the horse's sides. These are all normal and instinctive reactions, but the wrong ones. You must go against instinct, and RELAX.

Start again. If your horse is not wearing a neckstrap, take the reins in one hand (the outside hand if you are in an arena) and put the fingers of the other hand under the pommel. Don't press down on the pommel, that will tend to push your seat up. Now, head up, shoulders squared, sit deeply in the saddle but don't tense the muscles of your buttocks. Keep your thighs lightly against the saddle, relax your knee joints, let your lower legs hang down naturally — and forward you go into trot . . . one . . . two . . . one . . . two. Feel the rhythm, don't resist it. The moment you think you are going to lose balance, *relax* your muscles, lengthen your legs, soften your seat, feel play in your hip joints. Of course there is more 'punch' in the horse's movement; accept it, go with it. The less you try, the easier it will be.

22

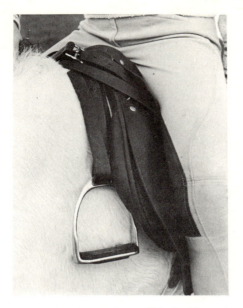

When riding without stirrups, if the buckles get in your way, pull them down from the 'bars' before you cross the stirrups, so that your legs can lie flat and comfortably against the saddle.

Whatever you do, don't hang on to the reins; grab the horse's mane if you must and there's no neckstrap; but the fingers under the pommel will help you. When you change direction, change hands on reins and pommel.

The best way to learn to trot is on the lunge, but failing that, persevere, with neckstrap and/or pommel holding until suddenly, it will feel comfortable and you will wonder what all the fuss was about. A good instructor, before teaching you to 'rise', will probably have you sitting to the trot without your stirrups. This is often easier than riding with them, because you have to stretch your legs down, which helps to keep your seat down. There is nothing better than the sitting trot, with and without stirrups, to improve, deepen, and strengthen your seat.

The rising trot is a forward, rather than an up-and-down

movement. Keep your ankle supple, put pressure on to the ball of your foot down from the inside of the knee, don't let your lower leg come forward. Feel the swing of the hindquarters, and let them give you a slight lift off the saddle, forward on to your thighs, on alternate strides. Once you feel the 'lift', try to keep it regular; saying 'one-two' to yourself is better than saying 'up-down'. Don't try too hard. If you lose the rhythm of the rise, sit, and start again. Don't try to push your seat up in the circular movement called 'stirring the porridge'! Your lower leg must stay in position. If it comes forward it will push your seat back, you will be behind the movement, and in an impossible position to rise correctly. If you keep the feeling of pressure from the inside of the knee down to the ball of the foot, ankle supple, heel slightly depressed, and your hips supple, to follow the movement, it is the punch of the hindquarters that will give you the rise: the horse will do the work for you.

The rising trot is a knack. Once you get it, you never forget it. To some people it comes easily and naturally; others, possibly those with less sense of rhythm, take quite a long time to achieve it.

To perform the rising trot well, however, is not so simple.

First: to keep the horse going forward evenly, the legs must do something. The only time they can 'ask' is the moment when you are sitting; each time you sit, the lower legs should squeeze against the horse, asking it to maintain speed and rhythm. The legs should always remain in contact with the horse's side, even as you rise to the trot.

Second: when trotting, the horse does not 'nod' its head; its head is steady, therefore your hands must be steady too. At first this is not easy; your hands will tend to wave about, conveying all sorts of extraordinary messages to the horse. As you progress and can carry your hands steadily at trot, they must begin to exercise control. If your legs are asking for an even, energetic trot, and your reins are slack, with no contact, all the energy the horse is producing will disappear 'out of the front door', as it were, rather as if you were driving a car in neutral. The horse will be 'on the forehand' and the trot uncontrolled to the extent that the horse will find it difficult to obey if you want to change direction, or bend.

Third: although your hands must be steady, they must not be 'fixed', nor your fists tightened into a hard, insensitive clench. The fingers of your rounded fists must be able to open and close, according to whether your want to increase or decrease speed.

It is also not so easy to keep the rhythm and speed of trot when changing from rising to sitting, as there is a slight change in your position. It is good practice to go from sitting to rising, to sitting, and rising again, trying to keep speed and rhythm regular. In a good trot, the horse's hindquarters should impel it energetically and rhythmically forward into the rider's controlling hand.

Once the rising trot has become established and easy, it is time to think about which diagonal you are rising and sitting on. Obviously, it is possible do so on either of the diagonals on which the horse's legs come to the ground. At first, you will have been pleased enough to 'get the rise' to bother about this; now, try to get the correct diagonal.

When you are circling, or going round an arena, to the right, you should be on the *left* diagonal; that is, sitting when the outside foreleg (the left one) is on the ground. When circling or going round to the left, you should be on the *right* diagonal; sitting when the outside (right) foreleg comes to the ground. At first, check this by looking at the horse's shoulder. After a time, you will be able to feel the diagonals without looking. If you see that you are on the wrong one, sit for one bump, and correct it. Check that you have actually done so. It is easy to sit for two bumps by mistake and be back where you started. When riding out, don't always sit on the same diagonal; if you do, your horse will become stiffer to one side than the other. A horse whose rider knows about diagonals will feel equally comfortable on either. By no means all horses do!

To go from walk to trot, shorten the reins, or, if your horse is walking on good contact, close your fists; press down with your seat, squeeze hard with both legs, and THINK of trot. Do not throw the reins at the horse; do not take your seat out of the saddle, and don't try to rise before your horse has begun to trot. To come back to walk, sit, if you have been rising — close your fists, keep your legs close to the horse's sides (the legs can 'hold' as well as ask for forward movement). As you check with your hands, change your own body rhythm from two to four and go *forward* into walk.

Practise going from walk to trot, and from trot to walk, until you can go smoothly from one gait to the other, always thinking of going *forward* into the slower gait: the downward transition.

The canter

The canter is a comfortable and enjoyable gait. Don't be frightened of it, thinking it means the horse is going to charge about faster and faster, leaving you helpless and probably yelling for help.

The canter, even a fast canter, is essentially a collected, or controlled, gait, not necessarily faster than an energetic trot, the extra impulsion from the horse's quarters flowing rhythmically into the rider's controlling hand. It is however a *different* gait, in that its rhythm is three-time: waltz time. If you remember this, and allow your body to accept it, you will find it easier to sit down to the canter than it was to learn to sit to the trot. There is a distinct forward thrust felt from the hindquarters at the start of each canter stride. If your seat is down and your loins relaxed, you will feel this giving your seat a slight forward-sliding movement with each thrust, which must be absorbed by your loins and hips.

A mistake which is often made when learning to canter — and often long afterwards — is to lift the seat out of the saddle and lean over the horse's shoulder, possibly to see which leg it is leading on. As the horse has to swing its shoulders forward when cantering, it doesn't help it if the rider's weight is on them. Another mistake is to have too long a rein: no contact. The result is that when the rider asks the horse to go forward more

Above Here, the rider has asked her pony for a canter to the right, off-fore leading; but has been a bit worried; will it take the correct lead—? but having looked down to check (unecessary), and found it has . . .

Above right . . . she has straightened herself, seat back into the saddle, taken up rein contact, and is cantering happily on. This picture shows the moment when the near-hind is thrusting, the off-hind and near-fore about to come forward together; the next phase will be the 'lead' of the off-fore, shown in the first picture, which will then be followed by the 'moment of suspension', when the sequence will start over again.

energetically, hoping it will canter, all it will do is trot faster and faster.

If you remember that in order to canter, a horse has to change the order in which its legs come to the ground, you will realize that you must 'prepare' it: give it advance notice of what you want it to do. You shorten the reins, or close the fists if already on good contact, you check, rather than increase, the speed of the trot, and then ask for the necessary change-of-leg sequence.

The best way to learn to go from trot to canter is on a bend; the horse is most likely to strike off with the correct leg leading. You will remember that on a bend to the right, it should 'lead'

27

with the off-fore; to the left, with the near-fore. A few strides before you come into the bend, sit to the trot, take a good contact, either shortening the reins or closing the fists; sit upright, seat in the saddle; as you round the bend, slightly check the speed of the trot and then ask firmly with both legs; the inside one close to the girth, the outside one a little behind it. Don't throw the reins at the horse; keep contact. The moment you feel the change of rhythm, go with it; but *don't lose your contact*. If you don't succeed the first time, don't go rushing off into a wild trot; check your speed, come back to a controlled, even trot, and think. You can't have made your aids clear enough to your horse. Perhaps when you checked your trot in the bend, you lost contact and let the horse's impulsion die away; you must feel its hindquarters active under you, your hand controlling the impulsion, not letting it escape. Or perhaps without knowing it you took your seat out of the saddle at the moment you asked with your legs. Try again on another bend. The first few times you succeed in cantering, just sit relaxed, feeling the new rhythm, and enjoying it. Then, begin to think.

At trot, the horse's head is steady. At canter, the head makes a slight movement with each stride. Your hands must be aware of this. If they are 'fixed' and your arms rigid, the horse will either fall back into trot, or take a firm hold against your hands and go faster and faster. The canter is essentially a controlled, collected gait. To keep an even speed, at each stride your legs should ask imperceptibly for it to be maintained, your hands holding and allowing alternately. Even when out hacking, when you may want to canter quite fast, you should keep your seat in the saddle. Only much later, when or if you want to jump or go fast across country, will you come forward into the Italian, or forward, canter. The Italian or forward canter position is referred to in the USA by a variety of terms: galloping position; jumping position; two-point; half-seat; and forward seat. Then, with shortened leathers, you take your weight off the saddle (but not your seat right out of it), carrying your weight on the inside of your thighs and knees, down to the ball of your foot.

To go from canter to trot, close and tighten your fists, bring your elbows a little back, stop 'asking' with your legs, close and hold them against the horse's sides; *don't lean back*, check firmly with your hands and then go *forward* into trot; the change of gait should be smooth, and the smoothness will depend on how quickly you can change your body rhythm. At first, it is much easier to come back into rising rather than sitting trot.

When you can canter comfortably and easily, practise cantering for a certain number of strides; then coming back to trot; then cantering on again for a different number before you trot. You can also practise increasing and decreasing canter speeds. To increase, allow a little more with your hands as your legs ask; then close the fists, and hold; then allow again for a few strides, then come back. These exercises will give you a feeling of confidence. When you are really confident, practise some cantering without stirrups. This will counteract any tendency you may have developed to lean forward, round your shoulders, or take your seat out of the saddle.

The gallop

The true gallop, when the horse is fully extended, head, neck and body stretched to their full length, and the beat of the stride four, is not a gait for any but the experienced rider. The least loss of balance on the part of the rider will upset that of the horse, and many even cause it to fall. At the gallop, the rider, with shortened leathers, takes his weight off the horse's back and loins, carrying it on the inside of the thighs and knees down to the ball of the foot. It is very easy for an inexperienced rider to lose control at the gallop, partly because of the sensation of great speed, which will make him hang on to the reins and come even further forward, which will encourage the horse to go faster, partly because it is not so easy to stay in balance. Feeling insecure, unbalanced and out of control may cause him to panic, and forget everything he ever learnt about how to sit on, and control, a horse.

Bending, circling and changing direction

It may sound a contradiction in terms to say that a horse should remain straight when bending, going on a circle, or changing direction. It isn't, because what is meant by a horse being 'straight' is that its hind feet are following directly into the track of its forefeet, not swinging out to one side or the other.

Now, the horse has a long body. If the hind feet are to follow the tracks of the forefeet when bending, the horse must bend its whole body, not just look the way it is going. Also, if it is to maintain speed and rhythm on bends, the hindquarters must be 'engaged', must be really working, to keep the horse going actively forward. To bend correctly, the horse must first look in the direction it is to go, the neck and the body then follow the curve of the bend, the outside hind leg making of necessity a slightly longer stride than the inside one. To get this result, the rider should think always of pushing the horse into a bend, not of pulling the horse round it.

How? Take a bend to the right. How are you going to get the horse to look to the right without pulling on the right rein?

Sit up, head up, looking ahead. As you come into the bend, look to the right yourself, and bring your right (inside) shoulder slightly back, and your left (outside) one, slightly forward. If you have started with an even contact on both reins you will not need to move your hands: the movement of your shoulders will have moved them enough; you will notice as you do this that you can just see your horse's right eye. At the same time, close your right leg firmly against the horse, on the girth; the horse will feel this pressure as a pivot, helping it to bend; and bring your left (outside) leg a little back. This will prevent the hindquarters swinging out, and help the outside hindleg to follow the track of the outside foreleg. Although you have moved your shoulders, you must not move your *seat* sideways: sit square. The different position of each leg will slightly alter the pressure on your seat bones, which will be felt by the horse.

Briefly, whichever way you are bending or turning, sit up, head up. Look right, or left; inside shoulder goes slightly back, outside one, slightly forward; inside leg on girth, outside leg behind it. Ride forward and try it first at walk. If you can do this calmly and correctly, you will be surprised how easily the horse will bend and how little you have had to do with your hands. If you pull on the inside rein instead of driving the horse forward between both reins, you will check the impulsion, the horse will give you a head and neck bend only, the quarters will swing out and the bend will be 'flat' and incorrect.

If you are simply making the bend at the end of an arena, the moment you are round it, straighten head and shoulders again, legs back into normal position. If you want to circle, keep in bend position. It may happen on a circle that you feel your horse 'leaning in'; leaning to the inside and making the circle smaller. This is probably your fault; you have collapsed all your weight on to your inside hip, maybe thinking you're helping the horse. In fact, with too much of your weight to the inside the horse has to lean in to keep his balance. Stop, and sort yourself out. Whatever movements you make with your head, your shoulders, and your lower legs, you must sit squarely in the saddle. If your seat is soft and your loins supple, the slight difference in your balance as you ride into turns and bends will of itself affect the pressure exerted by each seat bone without you, at this stage, having to worry about putting more pressure on one than on the other, provided you are sitting straight.

It is not easy to check for oneself that one is sitting absolutely straight: seat square and shoulders level. It is a good idea now and then to get someone to stand behind you and tell you if you are straight; not tilting your weight to one side or the other, and if your shoulders are level; not one higher or lower, or further back or forward, than the other.

First steps in jumping

While serious, or competitive, jumping deservedly has a book to itself, and is in any case not the ambition of every rider, anyone who becomes competent enough to ride out into the countryside will sooner or later find themselves having to get to the other side of small obstacle; perhaps a fallen tree trunk, or a ditch, or a gap in a hedge or wall into a wood. Anyone with good balance and a bit of nerve can get over this sort of thing somehow, but it will be a matter of good luck rather than good management. It will be much easier for both horse and rider if the rider has some idea what it feels like to 'leave the ground', and how to sit a jump without jabbing the horse in the mouth, or jarring its back by coming down with a bump when landing.

Jumping begins with walking, and then trotting, over poles on the ground. Starting with one pole, the rider approaches it at walk, aiming for the centre of the pole, looking up and keeping the walk strides of the horse even and true. The pole is then taken at rising trot. Again, the rider must look up and ahead, aiming for the centre of the pole, keeping the trot rhythm even, the hands in contact, 'allowing' as the horse trots over the pole but not throwing the reins at the horse.

Next, three, four or more poles, set between 4 ft 6 in and 4 ft 9 in (1·4-1·5 m) apart, depending on the size of the horse. 4 ft 6 in is the average. This is not quite so simple. At walk, aiming for the centre of the line of poles, the rider must look up, give slightly with the hands, keep the seat in the saddle but with supple loins, follow the lengthened strides of the horse. At trot, there will be an immediate temptation to look down; this must be resisted. Coming in to the line of poles at rising trot, the rider should look up and ahead, be ready to 'allow' with the hands, keep the lower leg in correct position, feeling pressure from the inside of knees and thigh on to the ball of the foot, and with supple loins, follow, and accept, the strong thrust of the hindquarters as the horse strides energetically and rhythmically over the poles. If the horse is doing this exercise well, the rider will feel a distinct rounding of its back under him. After trotting over the poles, trot on, go round and trot over them again, trot on, change direction and trot over them the other way round. It will soon be found that to do this exercise correctly, and comfortably, the muscles that hold the body upright (the stomach muscles) must work, if the body is not to collapse, the lower leg come forward, and the rider get 'left behind'. On a reliable

Nicely in control downhill through the beechwoods.

Ready for the lesson.

Left Cantering on through a forestry track among heather and pine trees.

Arm swinging. Notice how the eyes follow the movement of the hand.

Touching the toe; the rider's body is supple and the pony is going forward.

Walking over ground poles without reins.

horse this exercise can be practised with the reins knotted, the rider first holding a neckstrap, and then with arms folded.

The next stage is to put a small jump, about 18 in (0·45 m) high, or a cavaletto at its highest, at a distance of 9 ft (2·7 m) from the last trotting pole.

The rider comes in at rising trot, weight well balanced, lower leg in position, pressure from inside the knee and thigh on to the ball of the foot, and, looking up and ahead, with tummy muscles braced but supple loins, follows the thrust of the horse as it makes a small 'pop' over the tiny jump. The hands should stay in contact, but allow deliberately, coming forward to either side of the horse's neck. Again, on a reliable horse, this exercise can be practised without reins.

Now can come variations, and a slight increase in height and width of the jumps. Leave the first little jump as it is. On the other side of the arena or schooling paddock put a 2 ft (0·61 m) spread: 2 ft high and 2 ft wide. On a diagonal, or in the centre, put a small 2 ft jump that can be taken in either direction. Two straw bales laid lengthwise on their sides, with a pole on top, make a good and simple one. The rider can now shorten the stirrups by one hole (this is enough, as the jumps are very small)

Trotting without reins, at rising trot. Notice how freely the pony is going when allowed to use its head and neck to balance itself. The rider's lower leg is a little too straight; her toe has come in front of her knee, and her heel is not in line with her seat, but she is looking up and ahead.

and trot round the arena or paddock, avoiding the jumps. When ready, the horse going evenly and the rider comfortable, the rider goes into the first small jump, and poles, at trot; carries on, turns towards the little spread, and still in trot, goes over it. Trot on, change direction, take the straw bales and the spread the other way round; change again, re-take the bales, and finish with the small first one. Rest . . .

If after the spread the horse takes a canter stride, bring it quietly back to trot. This exercise can also be done without reins by making a knot in the reins, riding the bends with the hands on the reins in front of the knot, letting go and folding the arms when in line with the jump, picking them up again for the trot on and direction change. When this can be done correctly, you can say the rider knows what it feels like to 'leave the ground'.

It is important to begin jumping out of trot, and over very small obstacles, because it is only when going slowly that the rider has time to feel exactly what is going on underneath him

Above Super jump from the pony, with head and neck free. Although the rider hasn't taken her seat out of the saddle, she has slipped back on it because she has rounded her back and hunched her shoulders instead of bracing her back and her tummy muscles, and carrying her weight on the insides of her thighs and knees. Her stirrups are rather long. If we did this exercise again it would be much better; this is really to show what happens if you don't 'prepare' yourself for even a tiny jump.

Above right Shoulders still hunched, so the hands couldn't come forward; notice they have lost the 'line', elbow-wrist-horse's mouth. The seat is unnecessarily far out of the saddle.

when a horse jumps, and how the body must work in order to follow the extra thrust of movement. If jumping is begun at canter, the rider will be tempted to come too far forward, taking the seat right out of the saddle before the jump: jumping before the horse, as it were. This can be disastrous. Should the horse stop, the rider will take the jump and not the horse! The seat should remain in the saddle until the moment of take-off, when the forward and upward thrust of the hindquarters will give it the necessary lift, provided always the lower leg is correct, pressure from inside knee and thigh on to the ball of the foot, enabling the rider's body-weight to follow the horse's upward and forward spring. It is also easier at trot to learn the correct following movement of the hands, which must follow the stretch of the horse's head and neck to either side of its neck: not upwards as though the rider was trying to touch its ears. The line from elbow through wrist to horse's mouth should always remain true.

Now for a jump out of canter. Put the small one in the centre of the arena, with only one pole 9 ft (2·74 m) in front of it. On one side, put a jump of about 2 ft (0·61 m), or a little more. Straw bales can be used again; this time, lay them flat, and make the jump of two bales high. Put a pole on the ground about 1 ft (31 cm) away from the base of the bales on either side. On the other side of the arena, put two jumps of not more than 2 ft 3 in (0·7 m) in height 22 ft (6·5 m) apart. Now, work in at trot, then trot down over the small centre pole and jump; at the end of the arena bend first towards the side with the single jump, canter on, and down over it; canter on, and take the small double. There will be one non-jumping stride between the two elements. Then, the first time, come back to trot, to walk, and rest.

The small double gives excellent practice in continuing to follow the horse after it has jumped; not collapsing and thinking 'thank goodness we're over that one!'

Cantering in to small jumps, the seat is not taken out of the saddle, but it is not dropped down deliberately into it, as it is in the school canter on the flat. In the USA most instructors teach riders to approach a jump in a forward or two-point position, maintaining this over the fence. In canter, as in trot, there must be pressure from inside knee and thigh on to the ball of the foot, the loins must be supple, and the body ready to follow the jump athletically. It will be noticed by the rider that if the seat is not raised exaggeratedly, and the hands follow correctly, both seat and hands will more or less automatically come back into normal position on landing.

To improve confidence and to keep the rider always looking ahead, the little jump lay-out, or something similar, can be used

The rider has a much better position of hands and head, but she has slightly over-corrected her previous exaggerated 'bottoms up' angle. By not taking enough weight from knee and thigh on to the ball of the foot, her seat is a little too far back in the saddle. Her hands are better able to follow the stretch of the pony's neck, and she is now looking up and ahead to what comes next.

to make the jump-sequence longer. For example: trot up the centre; take the double at canter first; canter on, take the single jump, come back to trot, make a diagonal change of rein, re-take the double in reverse, out of canter, then the single, then back to trot, and either a diagonal change at trot, or trot past the double without jumping, back to walk, let the horse go on a long rein, stretch and relax, then halt and rest.

A rider who can cope correctly and confidently with small jumps out of both trot and canter can feel competent to cope with any small natural obstacle that may be encountered on a ride. There is no need to go on practising endlessly. Although some pole, and small jump, work is an excellent suppling exercise for both horse and rider it should not be carried on *ad nauseam*; nor, by the less experienced rider, for too long without supervision and instruction.

4 Balance and co-ordination

When you start to ride, although it is fairly easy to learn what 'the aids' are, it is not so easy to put them into practice. While the basic principles of riding are balance, relaxation and rhythm, the technique of riding involves teaching one's body to use different parts of itself separately and individually, and yet to co-ordinate them.

You may well ask, how on earth can I be relaxed if I'm continually having to think of what to do with my arms and legs and seat and head and shoulders? The answer is, you can't; until your body begins to react more or less automatically; until you no longer need to think of what to do, but of how you are doing it. It's like learning any other sport. For a long time, a tennis player has to think of how to hold the racket for different shots, or how to stand when taking a backhand. Only when those reactions become automatic can he begin really to play.

The best way to teach your body what to do when riding is to do exercises on horseback. Do them on the ground as well if you like, to keep fit; but those done on a horse will help most.

To be relaxed and balanced on a horse, the first thing one has to do is unstiffen oneself. Free, and be conscious of freeing, all those joints and muscles and parts of oneself not used, or used without thinking, in ordinary life.

Start at the top: with the shoulders. Nearly everyone, particularly if they're round-shouldered, is stiff in the shoulders, having apparently forgotten that they have individual shoulder-blades, each capable of considerable movement.

Riding, you cannot use your hands correctly if your shoulder-blades are rigid, as though set in concrete. Your hands are the extremities of your arms; and your arms begin, not at the elbow, but at the shoulders.

To free your shoulders
Get a friend to hold your horse, or make a knot in the reins so that it doesn't start to eat grass while you're doing the exercise. Now, bring your elbows out sideways, and put your hands across your chest, finger tips touching. Rotate your elbows forwards and round, and feel your shoulder blades moving; if they're very stiff, you'll probably hear them creaking with the unwonted exercise. Now, rotate the elbows the other way round; first one elbow, and then the other. Keep your head up, and don't hunch up the points of your shoulders. Rest. Even after doing this once, you will feel taller and more erect. If when riding you feel your shoulders getting fixed and stiff, loosen them by imagining a fly has got stuck down your shirt between your shoulder blades; wriggle them, as though to dislodge it!

To check and/or correct the position of your seat and legs, improve your balance and supple your hips
Keep the friend holding your horse, unless it is willing to stand still a bit longer. Stand up in your stirrups. There is a right and a wrong way of doing this. First: if your legs are too far forward you won't be able to stand up at all. Second: don't use your hands to help yourself up. Put pressure on the inside of your knees down on to the stirrup on the ball of your foot, and rise forwards, your body in a slanting forward line; not with your behind stuck out and your shoulders hunched. The 'line' you make should be somewhat like that of a figurehead on an ancient ship. Head up, looking forward. Now, sit again; but don't collapse with your seat to the back of the saddle and legs stuck forward. Bend your knee and ankle joints: fold yourself back on to the saddle, as it were, keeping your lower leg exactly in position. Repeat, until you can do it easily. Now, next time you stand, put both arms straight out, shoulder level, and swing your body to the right, to the front, to the left, to the front; and sit. You will need to. A further elaboration of this exercise is: stand in your stirrups, then, without looking down or moving your body, take your feet out of the stirrups; hold the position

Above Standing in the stirrups.
Above right Arms shoulder level, body swing to the right, to the front, to the left, to the front; repeat several times. This picture shows distinctly how the weight is carried from the inside of the knee down to the ball of the foot, and how the body is swung from the hips, and the arms held level. Although this demonstrator is a child, it is perfectly possible for adults to do this exercise without either collapsing half-way through, or sticking out their rears, or cheating by leaning on the pommel!

a couple of seconds, then sit. This will let you feel exactly where your 'riding muscle' is: on the inside of your thighs and knees.

To supple your hips and help your balance

Keep the friend; or, if no friend is at hand, give the horse a bit of a trot before asking it to stand again. Knot the reins if no friend. Take both feet out of the stirrups. Sitting very straight, head up, swing your right leg over the front of the saddle so that you are in the position of a person riding side-saddle. Take care as this could startle your horse. *Swing* it; don't heave it over as though you had arthritis, and don't hit the horse's ears! Swing it back; repeat with the left leg. Keep your seat square and yourself sitting up, head up. Repeat several times. If you have a friend to help, you can turn this exercise into 'round the world': that is: right leg over the front, left leg over the

Above 'Legs over the front'... the leg should really swing over the withers, not touching, or resting on the back...

Above right However, here we are; it's got there! Any moment now, back it must swing, and the left leg have its turn!

back; right leg over the back, left leg over the front. This means a considerable swivelling of the seat. NEVER do this exercise unless someone is holding the horse. Swinging the legs alternately over the front is really just as good; it is after all rather pointless to sit back to front on one's horse.

To supple your hips, and develop your stomach muscles
Lean forward along your horse's neck, body stretched forward, head along the mane, looking up between the horse's ears, your lower leg kept in position. Sit up, then lean back, right back, dropping your head on to the horse's rump just above its tail, lower leg still in place. Again, do this with caution; have someone to hold the horse when you lean back! Raise yourself up again, without heaving about with your arms and legs; not as easy as it sounds.

The next exercises are best done on the lunge, because they should be done in movement, but you can do the first two on your own.

45

Above Forward, stretched along horse's neck, looking up and between its ears.

Above right Back, head resting on horse's rump. These two positions aren't difficult in themselves; it's getting back upright again without waving the legs about and heaving with the arms. The tummy muscles have to do a lot of work.

Arm swinging, to free arms and shoulders, and supple your hips
On the lunge: each arm alternately is raised upwards and forwards, fingers extended, then swung round in a circle, the rider watching the hand the whole way round. You can do this riding on your own by taking the reins in one hand and exercising the other arm; then reversing arm and rein hand when you change direction. Don't hunch up your shoulders as you swing your arm; and try to think of this as a rhythmic exercise.

Toe touching; to supple whole body and develop balance
If you are doing this on your own, try it first at halt. Take the reins in one hand, raise the other arm straight up, then swing it down and touch the toe on the same side. You will really have to bend your body to do this, and drop your head. Keep your outside leg in position, or you may find yourself in a position of no return. When you can do this stationary, try it at walk. Done on the lunge, it is usual to bend over and touch the *opposite* toe.

Balance pivoting on the hips
This exercise has to be done on the lunge as it involves both arms. Raise both arms out sidways, shoulder level; don't hunch the shoulders. Pivot the body round to the right; to the front; to the left; to the front. Keep the arms level; one will nearly always tend to drop.

If you are being lunged, you will be working with an instructor, who may well ask for other exercises. Different people have different problems and stiffnesses, which are helped by different exercises. An exercise which benefits everyone, however, is to ride on the lunge with the hands held in the position of carrying the reins. The odd thing is that many people who find it hard to keep their hands steady on actual reins, can keep them steady on imaginary ones!

Another good exercise is to throw a tennis ball, or something about the same size, from one hand to the other when walking or trotting on the lunge. In order not to drop it, you find yourself reaching forward, or sideways, so determined to catch it that you forget about your seat and legs which begin to ride 'of themselves'. Don't use an apple; if you drop it the horse will make a dive for it!

All the lunge exercises will be done first at walk, then at trot, sometimes with, sometimes without, stirrups. Finally, some will be done at canter.

Checking your position is in itself an exercise which you should do every time you ride, either when you mount, or at some time during the ride. Halt. Take both feet out of the stirrups, and feel yourself sitting deeply and squarely in the saddle. Now, stretch your legs down as far as they will go, taking your knees and thighs back, and down, your feet in natural position, the toes just raised. Now, stretch your body *up*; feel tall: head up, shoulders wide and open, not rounded. If you are wearing a collar, the back of your neck should touch it. Then, without moving your head or your body, flex your knee and ankle joints and take up your stirrups, and you should be sitting correctly: your hips (your seat) squarely under your shoulders, and your heels under your hips (your

Above Checking position. Sit centrally in the saddle, stretch the legs, relaxed, as far down as they will go, and stretch your body upwards: feel 'tall'.
Above right Then take your stirrups back, pick up your reins, and you will be sitting very nicely indeed.

seat). If this 'line' is correct, you will find you can stand in your stirrups with no difficulty, and no alteration of leg position.

Should the 'line' become incorrect, your heels in front of your seat and your shoulders behind it, you will be 'behind the movement'. If your legs come too far back, behind your seat, and your shoulders in front of it, you will be sitting on your fork, and be 'in front of' the movement.

Always think of riding tall: head up, shoulders wide, and eyes looking ahead, where you are going; not shoulders round, head poked forward, and eyes down, as though you were apologizing for being on a horse!

5 Enjoy your riding

Everyone should start learning to ride in an indoor school or an enclosed *manège*. It is far easier to try to do what your instructor tells you if you know that your horse is bound to stay within a restricted space.

The only exception is very small children, who nearly always get on better if they are taught on leading-rein ponies, led by mounted instructors. A small child finds it very difficult at first to steer even the best mannered pony round an arena, and at the same time listen to what he's being told to do with his seat and legs. Even if a riding school has a bevy of active helpers willing to lead, and run beside, the children, a mounted instructor leading a child will get far more over to him, far more quickly. The child feels more grown up, confident, and interested if riding alongside a horse, and more anxious to learn to do things properly, so that he can progress to being 'let off'.

Naturally, leading-rein ponies must know their job, which is to lead alongside the horse, neither pulling back nor pushing forward, nor shoving so close against it that the child's legs get squashed. Taught on a good leading-rein pony that goes freely beside a horse, the child will not feel the need to kick, bang and flap with his legs to keep the pony going, habits which once developed are hard to eradicate. Trotting will be learnt more easily because the child won't have to push the pony; the rising trot may happen naturally, the child imitating the instructor. The leading-rein pony should wear a neckstrap, so that the instructor can sometimes let the child ride without reins, taking them over the pony's head and carrying them with the lead rein. The child can ride with one hand on the neckstrap, then without hands; then, at walk, he can do simple arm exercises. Coming to a halt, the reins are given back, and the child taught to pick them up again neatly, correctly and quickly. It is fairly easy, from alongside, to judge when the child is secure and confident enough to be 'let off', for a short period the first time; a good leading-rein pony will not wander from its companion horse. As the child gains confidence, the instructor can halt and ask the child to ride a short distance away, then turn and come back; first at walk, then at trot. Then the child can halt, while the instructor walks on and halts, and watches how the child walks or trots up. Very good leading-rein ponies should also know how to canter, to the word, alongside the horse, so that the child's first canter can be achieved 'attached'.

Needless to say, very good leading-rein ponies are worth their weight in gold to any riding establishment or private person. Unfortunately, most riding schools today are so busy that few are willing to spend the time to teach a child individually this way. If you find one that is, it is worth paying extra for the service. If you are a competent rider, with a small child who wants to learn, it is worth your while spending a little more than you think a small pony should cost if it is guaranteed to be an exemplary leading-rein one, and teaching your own child this way.

To go back to adults and older children . . .

Although early lessons must always be given indoors or in an enclosed arena or paddock, to ride permanently indoors or in a *manège* is restricting both to horse and rider. There comes a time when every novice rider, if he or she is to develop, must get out, and ride out of doors. Only by riding out of doors can you learn to ride on uneven ground; to ride up and down slopes and hills; to ride through woods, ducking under low branches instead of getting swept off by them; to cope with traffic without becoming so tense that your horse automatically thinks something frightful must be about to happen — in short, to keep your balance and your cool in all circumstances.

Your instructor will know when you are ready to ride out, and if the school has its own land, or there are country rides available to it, will suggest that you do so. Many urban schools, however, have no outdoor facilities beyond a *manège* or a jumping paddock; you should then ask advice as to where to go, where you can be sure of being mounted according to your ability, on a reliable horse, accompanied by a reliable person, and given an enjoyable and instructional outing, either alone, or with other sensible riders. You do not want to be involved in some mad, uncontrolled helter-skelter.

Incidentally, however much your riding improves, whenever, or if ever, you ride somewhere new, or maybe go on a riding holiday at home or abroad, it is always sensible to be modest about your ability. Experienced people can assess this very quickly. It is better they should discover you to be more experienced than they expected, when you will be given a better horse next time or next day, than that you should be ignominiously demoted from an animal you can't control.

When you first ride out, away from the even and level ground of *manège* or school, you will probably be tempted to keep your eyes on the ground, and your hands busily trying to guide the horse, as though otherwise it might not know where to put its feet. This is quite unnecessary! The horse doesn't want to fall down any more than you want it to. It is perfectly capable of managing its own legs on uneven or rough ground. Look up and look ahead, so that you can see, and avoid, any pitfalls before you come to them: maybe a hole in the ground, or an exposed tree root. If you're driving a car, you don't keep your eyes on the bonnet; you look up and ahead, in the direction you're going. Do the same when you ride out. Besides, you won't see much of the country you're riding through if you spend your time looking at the ground.

Going up and down slopes and hills will also be unfamiliar. Slight slopes, up or down, are no problem. On uphill ones, keep your knees and ankles supple, your lower leg in position, and your balance well with the horse: don't get left behind. Downhill, shorten the reins a little, don't lean back; keep correct leg position, close the thighs against the saddle, and go with the horse, holding him on good contact. Going up a steep hill, you must take your weight off the saddle, and come right forward from the hips, letting your arms stretch forward on either side of the horse's neck. Watch a horse going up a steep hill, you will see that it needs to stretch his head and neck right out. You must therefore allow it to do this by letting your arms go forward, taking your weight out of the saddle, bringing your body forward. Down a steep hill, shorten the reins. Don't lean back. Close your thighs, keep your lower leg on; knees and ankles supple, heels depressed; brace your body and your tummy muscles, and try to feel that you are holding the horse against the weight of your body. It is important to hold an absolutely steady pace down a steep, or even moderately steep, hill; like ourselves, if a horse once starts going faster, it finds it more and more difficult to stop. Always ride straight down a steep hill. If the horse slips, all that will happen is that its quarters will slide underneath it. If it slips when you are going down sideways, it could roll over, and give both of you a disastrous fall.

Trotting and cantering up and down slopes are matters of practice; of keeping the rhythm and holding the contact even, and your balance always with the horse. Uphill, allow with your hands; downhill, hold on contact. Holding does not mean pulling. If your balance is with the horse, not resisting the forward movement, you will find you can hold, without pulling, against the weight of your body.

Riding through a wood, look out for low branches, and duck forward, over your horse's neck, when you see one coming. If you ever have to ford a river, don't look down at the current, look at the opposite bank. Always give your horse a chance to drink before you cross, and then drive it forwards and over. You don't want to stop in the middle, when the horse may think it rather fun to have a nice splash, possibly even decide it would like to lie down in the nice cool water! If you have to come out up a bank, give with the reins and arms, come right forward in the saddle, and be prepared for a fairly strong hoist from the horse's quarters.

Riding along a road or lane, ride on the verge if there is one; if not, as close to the side as possible. Keep your outside leg, that is your right leg, on more firmly than the inside one, giving the horse the feeling it is being ridden in to the left. Keep its head straight towards oncoming traffic; if you turn it inwards, it can swing its quarters out on to the road.

Trotting the poles freely and accurately.

Quite a nice small jump; the hands could have 'allowed' a little more.

Plenty of room to canter abreast on this grassy track. The dog enjoys it too.

Coming downhill; the rider is a little too far forward, too soon.

On the way home, through a gap in the hedge.

Coming to a river during a day's hack in Scotland.

Let the horses drink before crossing water.

Moving on refreshed. Rivers are best forded where the water is running fast over gravel — but always take local advice before crossing one you don't know.

Home through the heather. Don't canter on stony, uneven ground; your horse could slip or fall on a loose or rolling stone.

If a large vehicle approaches or comes up behind, and you would like it to slow down, most lorry drivers are considerate and will do so if you given them the slow down signal with your hand. Do remember to smile, or give a 'thank you' salute to drivers who have been thoughtful. Trot on, on roads, when you can see well ahead. Don't trot round bends on narrow ones; you never know what you may find round the corner.

Riding out, you will begin to learn country manners, which are important if riders are to retain their privileges of riding through the countryside; on bridlepaths or over land belonging to friendly neighbours. Always shut gates carefully, don't just hope they will swing to behind you. If you're on a 'bridleway', remember it is also a footpath, and people may be walking on it. If you see no one, you can canter on; but don't do so round a bend; you may come upon an elderly lady exercising her dog, or a mother with a bevy of young children. If you have to pass people walking, slow down to a walk yourself. If you were walking, you would not like to have a horse or horses charging past you, probably spattering you with mud if it's wet ground. When a right of way is shown as going across a field, use it if the track is obviously well used. If it isn't, it is more tactful to ride round the headland (that is, along the fence or hedge). Ride slowly through, or around, a field which has stock in it. In spring, even if you are riding through permitted land, keep out of fields where sheep are lambing, or there are young lambs. In the country, greet and acknowledge the people you pass. When the time comes that you have a horse or pony yourself, don't take it for granted that you can ride everywhere you may have ridden out with a riding school; they may have had special permission. Good neighbourliness is an important part of country life; it is polite to ask if you also may have the freedom of the land. If there is Forestry Commission land near you, you must ask for permission to ride through it. This is seldom refused, though you may be charged a small yearly amount for the privilege.

As well as country manners, there are 'riding manners'. If you're riding in a group, don't ride past someone without giving them warning, particularly if going fast. Say: 'coming up on your right — or left' — or whatever. When you come to gates, don't always let the same person do the opening and closing, especially if the rider has to dismount to do some of the gates. Ride through gates spaced out, not bunched up and pushing one another: the best-behaved horse can kick out if pushed and jostled from behind. Don't ride off until the gate is closed: if someone has had to dismount, wait until they have remounted. Always say 'thank you' to whoever coped with the gate, even if it's your best friend! While it's often possible to ride two or three abreast, enjoying each other's company, never entirely lose your riding concentration. Keep a part of your mind, however interesting the conversation, on your own horse. Don't ride up too close behind another rider. If you're in the front, and you want to change pace, to trot, canter, or even gallop on, give a signal of your intention to the others. They may be having a lovely relaxed gossip, and be taken disastrously unawares if you suddenly take off. Similarly, if you want to do something particular with your horse, maybe let it out across a stubble field, or practise going up and down a steep hill, warn the others who may or may not want to emulate you. If a group has to cross a road, one person should halt in the road, ready to slow down or stop traffic while the others cross, riding abreast not in a line, as quickly, and for once, as close together as possible. It is murder to straggle across even a minor road, with no one keeping a watch out for traffic.

Riding in a group is fun, provided everyone behaves considerately and unselfishly, and the riding is geared to the capabilities of the least experienced rider.

If there is a branch of the Pony Club, or a Riding Club, near where you live, it is worth joining even if you haven't yet got a horse or pony of your own. Both organize quite a few unmounted activities; besides, one can always learn a lot from watching others ride, at rallies or in competitions, and organizers are always grateful for enthusiastic unmounted help.

While many of today's most successful riders, in all disciplines, have graduated from the Pony Club, the Pony Club is not, and never has been, simply a nursery for the talented! Below the top layer of the specially talented, and well-mounted, there are literally thousands of children, in many countries, benefiting from the instruction, and enjoying the fun, offered to them by being members of a Pony Club branch. Provided parents don't interfere and try to push their children into being too competitive, joining the Pony Club can give a child a lot of pleasure, as well as a good grounding in horsemastership: one of the Pony Club's aims has always been to teach children how to care for their ponies.

If you're a novice rider, don't be put off from joining a Riding Club because you think you're not good enough, or your horse isn't good enough, to go in for competitions. There's no compulsion on anyone to compete, there are plenty of other activities in which you can take part, on a perfectly ordinary horse or pony. A lot of small adults ride ponies; they're easier and cheaper to keep and, except in official Inter-Club competitions, where the height must be over 14.2 hh, there's no minimum height limit on Riding Club members' mounts. Most clubs, like most Pony Club branches, have a top layer of ambitious riders. The main body of their membership, however, is of people who enjoy riding, the good fellowship of being with others who have similar interests, and the chance to benefit from occasional instructional rallies and courses. These rallies and courses are important parts of Riding Clubs' activities: first, because, organized by the Club, it costs less to take part in them than it would cost to take oneself and one's horse to a riding establishment; second, because they are usually arranged in sections, so that groups of riders of more or less the same standard can be taught together. Even if initially you feel a bit shy of taking part, go and watch. A great deal can be learnt by watching a good instructor take a class. Seeing how others ride, what their mistakes are and how those mistakes are corrected, helps you to develop a critical 'eye', and will probably encourage you to be brave, and take part yourself the next time.

If there's no Riding Club in your neighbourhood, you should take any opportunity that may be offered of having lessons from a good instructor. No one ever comes to the end of learning to ride; the more you improve, the more you will want to learn, because the better you ride, the more you enjoy it. If you do have lessons from different instructors, remember that although all good instructors are aiming for the same results, they may express themselves differently. If, therefore, one tells you to do something which you do not understand, or which to you seems to contradict something told you by another, don't just sit there looking glum and puzzled. Ask the instructor to explain further; say what you had previously been told, and you will probably find that both have been trying for the same thing but have asked for it differently.

As time goes on and your riding progresses, you may find that one discipline, or kind of riding activity, appeals to you more than another. Perhaps dressage; perhaps jumping, or riding across country, or long distance. If you have talent, time, and money enough to pay for specialized instruction, go ahead and concentrate on whichever one it may be. But in concentrating on one objective, try never to lose the relaxed pleasure you get from riding itself. Every horse and every rider benefits from a relaxation from specialization. So, don't spend all your time schooling, or practising madly for a competition. Your horse will become stale, and you so strung up that your riding will suffer, because you have forgotten how to enjoy it.

To parents with riding children — provided the children have trustworthy ponies and have learnt to be competent riders, if you live where they can go on long country rides, let them do so on their own. Give them a picnic and let them be away all day if they want to. It will develop their initiative and their feeling of companionship with their ponies. It is good for children to be allowed to be adventurous, and to learn to become self-reliant.

6 Choosing and caring for a horse

Riding progresses in stages. However much natural talent or aptitude you may have, you can't become a competent, confident rider in six lessons.

Everyone, adult or child, should learn to ride on sensible, reliable horses or ponies, which will put up with their riders constantly doing the wrong thing, and do their best to obey what will often be somewhat muddled commands. It's impossible to learn on young, unschooled animals, or on ones that are corn fed, hunting fit, excitable and temperamental. If a friend has such a horse, and kindly offers to teach you to ride on it, don't accept. You will be so 'over-horsed' that instead of learning to ride, you'll probably be put off riding for good.

To be 'over-horsed' means riding, or trying to ride, a horse you feel you can't control. This makes you, understandably, nervous and tense, so you lose confidence; the horse becomes nervous and tense too and loses confidence in you. The result: the horse becomes progressively more difficult, and you, progressively more nervous.

If your learn at a good school, this should never happen to you, because at each stage of your riding, you'll be mounted on suitable horses, which you can control. Good instructors know how to evaluate their pupils' capabilities. Naturally, they want you to progress; but they will never 'over-horse' you, because they don't want to undermine your confidence and possibly stop you riding altogether.

However, the time may well come when, having become a reasonably good rider, you want a horse of your own. Or, if it's your child who has been learning, you want to buy him a pony. It's obviously important that you should always get a veterinary surgeon to check that whatever animal you think of buying is sound. What is really even more important is to be sure that it is going to suit your, or your child's, riding ability.

Never, unless your child is exceptionally talented and can have constant expert supervision, buy him a young pony because it is cheaper, and you think it would be so nice for the two to grow up together. Because a child can manage a quiet riding school pony quite well this does not mean he knows enough to be able to handle, break and school a young one. The two will get in a hopeless muddle; the child will either lose his nerve or his temper, or both, and the pony will be spoilt. You wouldn't expect even a very bright five-year-old child to teach another five-year-old to read. To expect a child to learn riding, and a pony to learn how to be ridden, at the same time, is asking the blind to lead the blind with a vengeance.

A child's pony, particularly his first pony, should be sensible, reliable, and know its job, which is to help the child to learn to ride, and to give him confidence. It doesn't need to have a long pedigree or be madly good-looking; it can be quite elderly, when it will probably cost even less than buying an unsuitable youngster. It should also be easy to catch and handle because a great deal of the pleasure children get from ponies is from handling them, grooming them, riding them bareback to and from their fields. Conformation-wise, it should not be so broad that the child's legs stick out at either side. Some Shetlands are very broad; some are not, and if they have been properly broken and well-ridden by other small children, they make good first ponies. Welsh Mountain ponies are narrow, but often rather too excitable for first ponies; Dartmoors are equally narrow, and more suitable temperamentally. But really, it doesn't matter what breed a first pony is, or even no particular breed, provided it is quiet, reliable, and neither a slug nor a tearaway. It is far better for a child's future riding career to have a first pony that is willing, but needs pushing on, than one the child is not always sure of being able to stop or control. This is the equivalent of the child being 'over-horsed', and will end with him or her developing bad riding habits, and wanting to use extra contraptions: martingales, complicated nosebands, strong bits, possibly even a gag snaffle. No first pony should have to be ridden in anything but a plain jointed, or unjointed, snaffle, and a simple bridle with a cavesson noseband.

Where elderly ponies have the advantage over young ones is that many of them seem not only to like children, but also have developed a feeling of responsibility for small ones, standing still when they fall off and waiting patiently while they climb aboard again. They will allow their manes and tails to be experimented with endlessly; submit to being dressed up or taught tricks, and seem to enjoy teaching their children how to play gymkhana games.

You should never buy a first pony, or any other pony for a child, without the child both riding it, and handling it — putting its tack on and taking it off; leading it about on a headcollar, brushing it, and lifting and picking out its feet. Pony-mad children are not critical and will fall in love with any pony. Be very sure, therefore, before you actually buy one and bring it home, that it is the right one. If it isn't, and you have to get rid of it, there will be just as much fuss as though it had never put a foot wrong, or put the child off.

A good way to find ponies for children is to contact your nearest branch of the Pony Club; the Secretary, the District Commissioner, or the Chief Instructor. You are often wisest to ask your child's instructor to help choose a first horse or pony. Sooner or later, all children grow out of their ponies. If you go to one of the rallies, you will be able to see the pony working, and how its child rider manages it. If there is a branch in your neighbourhood, encourage your child to join.

When it comes to choosing a horse for yourself, assess your own riding ability honestly and critically. There is no point in buying a horse you think you will be able to ride next year. You want one on which you feel confident and relaxed *now*. If you're small and light, you don't need a big horse. In fact, it might be sensible to buy a pony which your child, if not too young, can also ride, or can grow into.

Remember, the bigger the horse, the more it will eat and the more it will cost to keep. Many adults ride ponies, or small horses, from 14.2 hh to 15 hh, and unless you want to go in for high-powered competitions, they will do everything that bigger horses will do.

If you're tall and light, then you do want a horse that will 'take up your legs'; but remember that height in itself is no particular advantage to a horse. A horse's 'performance': the way it goes and what its gaits feel like when you ride it depend on the way it is made, its 'conformation'.

If you're heavy, you need a horse able to carry weight, which is not necessarily a tall horse. The weight a horse is capable of carrying depends on its conformation: in particular, on the amount of its 'bone' in relation to its height and size. 'Bone' is the term used for the measurement of the cannon bone, taken just below the knee. Many tall horses have a relatively small measurement — light bone — for their height, and can therefore carry less weight than smaller, stockier horses with more circumference of the cannon. This is why native, or Mountain and Moorland, ponies can carry more weight for their height and size than lighter built, more finely bred ones; the larger breeds, Fell, Dales and Highland, more than many quite big horses. These three breeds make excellent mounts for the novice adult, or for the elderly, or for those who also work, and haven't time to give a big horse regular daily exercise. Thoroughbred or Arab first crosses of any of these make super mounts — if you can find them.

The Welsh Cob is also a weight carrier, but has become very fashionable, is a very successful driving horse, and therefore, expensive. There exist, however, many horses of no particular breed, but of 'cob type' ranging in height from 14.2 hh up to, and sometimes over, 15.2 hh. All are up to weight and most are sensible, free-going animals, fun to ride, and with a natural aptitude for jumping. A horse of cob type has a deep barrel; a well-rounded rib cage; powerful, rounded and muscular quarters, and relatively short legs; the forearm long, the cannon short, with good bone.

Unless you have become a very competent rider, and a knowledgeable horsemaster, have proper stabling, and are able to spend plenty of time looking after your horse as well as riding it, it isn't sensible to buy one with more than half Thoroughbred or Arab blood.

What breed or type of horse or pony you buy will also depend on how you intend to keep it. If it is to live out, then your choice must be restricted to a Mountain or Moorland, or a Mountain and Moorland first cross, or to a hardy type of cob which will grow a thick coat in winter. Even then, if you have no stabling, you will need a field shelter, which the horse can go into in bad winter weather, or away from the flies in summer, and where it can be fed, groomed and tacked up before riding. Unless you live in a very mild or warm climate, no horse with much Thoroughbred or Arab blood should be expected to be out at night in winter.

If you have stabling and a field, you have a far wider choice, because you can keep your horse on the 'combined system'. That is: out by day in winter, if not being ridden, and in at night; out at night in summer, brought in by day if and when you want to ride. Any horse or pony can live happily and healthily this way. A horse out by day in winter will probably need a New Zealand rug by day, and rugging at night. A pony or cob, unless you have it clipped or trace-clipped, will not.

If you have a stable and no field, and are working, it is really not sensible to keep a horse, unless you have a friend who can exercise it for you. A permanently stabled horse must have regular daily exercise if it is not to become a bored neurotic. Ponies are not happy permanently stabled; they need just as much exercise as horses, and must be very carefully fed to prevent them becoming grossly over-fat, and unfit.

When you go to see a horse or pony you think may be suitable, take a knowledgeable person with you, who can be impartial, and stop you making too hasty a decision. Obviously, you will want to ride the horse, but get the owner to ride it first. If anyone is to be bucked off, rather they than you. When you ride it, don't rush off into a fast trot; walk. Get the feel of the horse, and let it get the feel of you, a different rider. Does it relax to you, and you to it? Does it walk well, with a good stride and rhythm? A horse that walks well will usually ride well in all gaits. Trot, both sitting, and rising; change rein and see how it responds to the leg. When you feel in harmony, canter. Forget about the owner and the knowledgeable friend, think only of the horse. Ride it as well as you can, trying to assess its responses, and reactions to you. When you dismount, take it yourself back to the stable; untack it, handle it, see how it behaves in its box. Stand back and take a good look at it, try to assess it as a horse, not only as a ride. Don't worry about its conformation; your knowledgeable adviser will tell you what he or she thinks of that. What impression do you get of the horse's character and temperament? Do you, in fact, as an individual human being, like it as an individual horse? After all, if you buy it, it's you who will have to live with it, and it with you.

All of us who ride, or have to do with horses, obviously like them as animals, in the way dog lovers like dogs, and cat people, cats. Between you and the horse you buy, and which you are going to ride and look after yourself, there should, however, be a definite feeling of compatibility. A horse may give you a very good ride, and be quiet and easy to handle and yet not inspire you with the conviction that it is really the right one; one you're going to get on with, day in, day out; in the saddle and out of it.

Horses are as individual as people, each with its own temperament, character and, like ourselves, character quirks. All experienced horsey people know this, although they don't often put it into words. Those professionally connected with horses naturally have to work with all kinds of temperaments and characters; some easy and straightforward, some difficult. While they will be able to ride and handle them all, there will always be particular animals with which they are in greater accord, get on better, and like better. They won't necessarily be the easy, straightforward ones, either. Even the best and most successful competitive riders, who can ride any horse, know that outstanding horse-human partnerships only come into being when horse and rider are in accord and sympathy. Not even very good riders can get the best out of every horse. Those who can are, deservedly, world champions.

Temperament is of the first importance; not only the horse's: your own. If you are highly strung, inclined to be nervous, and get uptight in crises, you should not buy a highly strung, nervous, uptight horse. You need a calm, sensible one which will never undermine your confidence; the horse, a calm, sensible rider to build up its confidence. However, feeling a horse has the right temperament to go with yours does not altogether explain why, ride and looks being equal, you should feel more drawn to one horse than another. Perhaps it is because the horse also feels drawn to you, maybe by your voice or the way you handle it, sensing in you someone upon whom it can rely. Horses do not show liking for people in the same way dogs do; they show it negatively rather than positively, by acceptance and willing obedience. They can nevertheless distinguish between persons, and can very definitely show their dislike of those in whom they have neither trust nor confidence; those who are rough, quick-tempered, shout at them and treat them, probably because they are frightened of them, as though they were dangerous zoological specimens.

Mutual confidence is probably the answer. Not only must you like your horse, it must accept you. Therefore, even if the horse isn't exactly the animal you set out to buy, maybe the wrong colour, or bigger or smaller, if there's something about it, and between you and it, that makes you feel this is 'the one', buy it; provided of course your veterinary surgeon tells you it is sound. You will always regret buying a horse you like only with reservations, particularly if it is to be your one and only; your companion as well as your mount.

Tack
A well-made, comfortable saddle enhances the pleasure of riding. As most people who ride purely for pleasure can afford only one saddle, the best type to buy is the 'general purpose'. This saddle has a deep seat, in which it is easy to sit in the correct position. It is not so exaggeratedly forward-cut as a

jumping saddle; the knee rolls are not too pronounced and it has a neat, soft, thigh roll. It is made with a 'continental' panel; that is, the panels are not padded, but made of two layers of leather, allowing the rider's legs to lie close to the horse's sides. The pommel can be straight, half-cut-back, or cut-back. The halfcut-back is sensible, because it is more likely to fit different horses, with different heights of withers; buying a new horse need not necessarily mean buying a new saddle.

Obviously, the saddle must be comfortable for the horse as well as the rider. To fit the horse, the saddle should lie true along its back; the 'channel' or 'gullet', the space betwen the padding, wide enough to allow no pressure on the horse's spine. There should be plenty of clearance between the pommel and the withers. Standing behind the saddle, it should be possible to see daylight right through, from back to front.

Saddles are made in three widths of tree: narrow, medium and wide. A saddle that is too narrow for the horse will 'sit up' on its back, pinch its sides, and shift in position when ridden on. Too wide a saddle will 'sit down', with little or no clearance at the withers. As a very rough guide, the average riding horse will take a medium tree; the cobby types, or the larger Mountain and Moorland breeds, a wide one, and Thoroughbreds, a narrow. But horses vary within each breed or type. The only way of making certain a saddle fits is to try it on.

Many reputable saddlers will allow a saddle, or saddles, to be taken 'on approval': some will actually bring saddles to the buyer, and advise as to their fit.

However well a saddle fits a horse, before buying it the rider should mount and sit on it: not only to be quite certain that it's comfortable, but to check that the added weight does not alter the fit. When trying on a saddle, put a clean cloth or stable rubber under it, to keep it clean; but don't try it on with a numnah. A saddle should fit properly without a numnah, whether or not one is to be used subsequently.

Saddles are made on rigid, and on spring, trees. Spring trees are usually a little more expensive, but for anyone who does a lot of riding, they are worth it for the extra comfort the slight resilience gives to the rider's seat. There is no difference in comfort for the horse.

Saddles should always be bought from reputable saddlers. It is a great mistake to fall for something very cheap, with no maker's name. This sort are usually of eastern manufacture, badly put together, on mis-shapen trees; when they begin to fall apart, no good saddler will, or can, repair them. On the other hand, there is no need to buy the most expensive saddle on the market. Moreover, a second-hand saddle that has been well cared for is a very good buy, the advantage being that the leather is already soft and 'ridden in'. Saddlers often get saddles in to sell for clients who have changed horses and need different ones; it is always worth keeping a look out for one.

A new saddle needs a great deal of softening, particularly the underside of the leather, which will absorb quantities of neatsfoot oil. Because saddles are so expensive, they should be properly cared for. Never put them away wet. Wipe them over with a damp sponge, then dry them with a dry cloth, then apply saddle soap liberally. Keep a check on the padding, or stuffing. After about a year, a new saddle should go back to the saddler for this to be checked; it will usually have firmed down considerably, and may need padding on either side of the gullet.

There are many different kinds of girth. Three popular leather ones are: the three-fold girth, which has a rounded edge which is placed towards the front; the Balding, which is cut and shaped where it goes behind the elbow; and the Atherstone, which is stitched and shaped. All leather girths are good, but must be kept clean and soft. Webbing girths are always used in pairs; they are good, but frequent washing to keep them clean can weaken the fabric, which can snap right across, without warning! The best webbing girth is the Fitzwilliam. This consists of one very wide webbing band, with two buckles at each end, and one narrower band, which goes up the middle, running through small strips of leather near the top on each end of the wide band. This gives the girth three buckle fastenings. When the middle band is tightened, there is hardly any friction on the edges of the wide one, which makes it very comfortable for the horse. It isn't always possible to buy these 'ready-made', but a saddler will make one to order.

Nylon girths are cheap, and easy to wash and dry. But they have no elasticity, and tend to unflatten, turning into bunches of nylon string, cutting into the horse. The best for owner riders, and the easiest to keep, are lampwick girths. These are soft, easy to wash, and the girth has two buckles. Even if allowed to get dirty, the lampwick never seems to become hard; and being tubular, the edges are always soft against the horse.

Stirrup leathers should always be of good quality, their length bearing some relation to the length of the rider's legs. No one wants a yard of extra leather trailing down; nor, on the other hand, to run out of holes if someone with slightly longer legs has a ride on one's horse. Leathers should be kept clean and soft so that when their length is adjusted from the saddle, they slip easily through the stirrup bars. When cleaning them, it is a good plan to change them over, left to right, each time. If the left leather is always on the same side it will become stretched by the pressure of mounting and it will be difficult to get both an even length. The most important part to clean is the fold in which the iron lies. Acid from the metal eats into the leather; if it is not thoroughly cleaned off, in time it will rot the leather and may cause it to break suddenly.

Irons should be fairly heavy, made of stainless steel or solid nickel, and be about an inch (2·5 cm) wider than the rider's booted foot. Too light or too narrow irons are dangerous. Should the rider fall, they may make it impossible for the foot to free itself. Because the 'roughing' on the sole of irons wears down fairly quickly, it is comfortable — and warmer in winter — to ride with treads, made of ridged rubber, fitted into the space on the sole of the iron.

Bridles vary enormously in price and in quality. The most expensive are the show-type ones, made of high quality, narrow leather, with neat stitched nosebands. The cheapest, like the cheapest saddles, should be avoided as they will be made of inferior leather. For ordinary use, a straightforward bridle of medium width leather, with a plain cavesson noseband, is the most suitable, and will cost about midway between the cheapest and the most expensive. There is a great variety of reins; but, except for jumping or riding across country, no need to use anything but plain leather ones, about an inch (2·5 cm) wide, or plaited leather ones of the same width. These cost a bit more, but are easier to hold in wet weather. There is no need to lay in a lot of extras: drop nosebands, or martingales; better to wait and buy them when — or if — your particular horse needs them.

An eggbutt snaffle is the most usual bit, and one in which most well-schooled horses and ponies will, or should, go kindly. Some prefer a German snaffle, which has a thicker, and therefore milder, mouthpiece, and which can be either loose-ring, or eggbutt. A Fulmer (Australian loose-ring) snaffle has cheekpieces which prevent the bit slipping to one side or the other. A young horse often goes better in an unjointed snaffle with a slightly curved mouthpiece (mullen-mouthed): made of rubber, vulcanite, or metal. The more complicated bits, the Pelham, and the bit and bridoon of the double bridle, should not be used by riders until they have passed the novice stage, and have learnt to handle two reins. The exception is the Kimblewick, which is a very modified and mild type of curb/snaffle combination. The mouthpiece has a port, the rein-ring is D-shaped, and although a curb chain is worn, the bit is used with a single rein. This can be a very useful bit, particularly for headstrong ponies. It is called a Kimberwick in the USA.

Whatever the type of bit, it should fit the width of the horse's mouth. On average, a 15 hh to 15.2 hh horse takes a $5\frac{1}{2}$ in (14 cm) bit; but horses' mouths vary. Specially narrow bits are made for Shetlands, and the smaller native ponies.

A headcollar is necessary, for tying the horse in its box when being groomed, and for leading it; also a rope with a clip-end. Leather ones are now very expensive; nylon ones are satisfactory, easily washed, and cheaper. A halter, made of rope or webbing, is useful for leading, but is not practical for tying up, because a horse can learn how to slip it off.

A lot of people ride with numnahs, possibly because they see so many doing so that they think it must be 'the thing to do'. If a saddle fits a horse, there should be no need for a numnah, except on a young horse, or one that has a 'cold back', hunching its back up when it feels the cold of the leather. If a numnah is used, as the saddle is put on, the numnah should be pulled well up into the pommel, so it does not press on the withers.

All tack should be kept clean, and in good repair. Stitching and buckles should be checked constantly and any necessary repair done at once. Everyone who owns a horse should have a spare pair of reins, a spare girth, and a spare pair of stirrup leathers. Never use very hot water for cleaning tack; tepid only. Don't *soak* it, clean it with a damp sponge, not a wringing wet one. And let it dry before putting on saddle soap, which should be done with as dry a sponge as possible. Tack that is clean, but wetly soapy, is a menace; in wet weather the reins will become a slippery mess, and the bridle probably leave dark soapy stains on the horse's head!

Stabled horses are going to need rugs. Today, there are many excellent kinds of quilted nylon rugs, which are lighter than the wool-lined jute ones, and can be washed — in a washing machine! In very cold weather, a clipped horse will need an under-blanket; possibly even two. As the quilted rugs have their own surcingles attached, when underblankets are used, a roller will be needed, to go over the top of the nylon rug, and keep the folded-back underblanket in place. There are also waterproof, New Zealand type, nylon rugs for outdoors; probably the original waterproofed canvas ones are the most weather resistant.

Various boots: brushing, tendon, Yorkshire and overreach, only really become necessary for competitive horses — and riders. Every horse owner, however, should possess bandages: a set of wool stable bandages, and a set of stockinette or crepe exercise ones, and a tail bandage. There are various leg protectors on the market, for travelling; they are quicker to put on than bandages, but more expensive, and bandages do just as well. One should also have a roll of gamgee tissue.

A rider confidently negotiating her choice of fence in a riding club one-day event.

Neither horse nor rider look very confident about this...

...but they got over it somehow... This was a bit more than either was really ready for; but it's fun to 'have a go', and confidence comes with experience.

Dismounting at the end of a ride. Loosen the girth a few minutes before unsaddling to let the horse cool off gradually.

Running up the stirrup irons. Always do this before leading your horse into its box.

Trees, water, sunshine, horses and your favourite dog... is there any better way of enjoying the nature around us than on horseback?

Feeding
The correct feeding of any domestic animal must be based on its natural feeding habits, because it is to them that its digestive system will be attuned. The horse is a grazing animal. In the wild, or at liberty, it is grazing more or less all the time. Its digestive system, therefore, is attuned to coping with small quantities of food fairly constantly. It is not, like our own, made to cope with one large meal, and then a long gap before the next one. The horse, for its size, has a small stomach, but large and copious intestines, into which the stomach, when about two-thirds full, continually passes the food for digestion.

Obviously, the domestic horse cannot eat all the time if we want it to work; wanting it to work, we have therefore to try to feed it as closely as possible to its natural feeding habits, if it is to stay healthy and not have digestive troubles.

So, the first rule for successful feeding is: little and often. This rule applies in particular to the concentrate, or energy, foods a working horse needs. If a horse is in hard work, needing a lot of energy food, it needs an increased *number* of feeds; not larger individual ones. Roughly, a horse's stomach can only cope with about 4 lb (1·8 kg) of concentrate food at one time. Supposing, therefore, that a racehorse in training is getting 16 lb (7·3 kg) of oats a day, it must get them in four feeds; not in one or two huge ones.

However, even spacing out the concentrate feeds into small quantities and feeding them often, isn't going to keep the horse's digestive system working. It needs something to keep it going in between; some substitute for the herbage which, in the wild, the stomach would be constantly passing through to the intestines. In domestication, unless the horse is out at grass, that substitute is hay.

Hay and grass are what are known as 'bulk' foods. A horse that isn't working can live, and thrive, on nothing but one or the other. But although both can keep it in health, neither is in effect productive of energy, nor can either replace the energy which the working horse expends on our behalf. Our business is to give it the right amount of energy food for the work we want it to do; and the right amount of bulk food to keep its digestion in order. It is not too difficult to work out how to do this if one knows how much total weight of food a horse needs, or would eat for itself, in twenty-four hours.

For example, and as a rough guide. A horse of 15 hh will need 25 lb (11·3 kg) of food. For bigger or smaller horses, add or subtract 1 lb (0·54 kg) for every inch (2·5 cm) of height.

If the horse is working, that total amount must be divided between bulk (hay or grass), and energy food (oats, barley, cubes, etc). A horse in light work, perhaps only an hour a day, will not be using much energy so it will not need much energy-producing food — say 5 lb (2·3 kg). This means that it must have 20 lb (9 kg) of either hay or grass, or a mixture of the two. If it is in harder work, being asked to jump, or taken on long rides, it will need more energy food; say, up to 10 lb (4·5 kg), when the bulk ration must come down to 15 lb (6·8 kg). The principle is that as one type of food is increased, the other must be decreased, so that the total weight intake remains the same.

If a horse is kept on the combined system, and is out at grass by night in summer, one can allow 12 lb (5·5 kg) for the grass it will eat. In the USA the quality of the grass varies tremendously and some pasture has almost no nutritional value. If it is also out by day except when it is being ridden, it will need no extra bulk ration; that is, no hay. In winter, however, because there is little nourishment in grass, one can allow very little for the grass it may eat when turned out in the daytime; during the mid-winter months it will in fact need hay in its field. A horse that is off work for any reason must have its energy food cut down, and its bulk food increased.

Naturally, horses, like people, vary. Some are very 'good doers' and will get over-fat on their full weight ration. Some are nervous worriers, using up energy even when not working, and will need more, particularly more bulk, if they are to stay in condition. But the weight for height guide is useful, and one cannot go far wrong using it.

Exactly how much, and what kind, of energy food a horse

needs depends not only on the work it is doing, but on its temperament, and on the ability of its rider.

Oats are without doubt the best energy-producing and energy-replacing food for horses. In the USA a combination mix of grains called 'sweet feed' is very popular. But they must be fed with care, especially to horses in ordinary work, ridden by the ordinary pleasure rider. While some horses can 'carry their oats', others will become so excitable as to be no longer pleasure rides. It is therefore not wise to feed them to children's ponies. Oats are best fed bruised. If fed whole, they are apt to be eaten too quickly, not properly masticated, and can go right through the horse still more or less whole.

Flaked or bruised barley is almost as high in nutritional value as oats, and yet for some reason has not the same 'exciting' effect.

There are many brands of cubes and, in the USA, pellets (very small cubes) on the market, and various kinds within the brands: ordinary horse and pony cubes; 'complete' cubes; racehorse cubes, with a high protein content; and stud cubes, specially balanced for brood mares and young stock. The advantage of cubes is that they do not, or should not, vary in quality or content. All the same, a steady diet of cubes, and nothing but cubes, must surely be very boring for the horse, as a diet of only one kind of food would be for us.

Bran is really a food adjunct; a little added to a feed encourages the horse to eat slowly and chew properly. It is also useful as a mash, when a little molasses (black treacle) added makes the mash particularly appetizing.

Sugar beet pulp, or cubes, is appetizing and helps to keep condition but must always be soaked before being fed.

Any kind of cake, or cube, made for cattle, should NOT be fed to horses, because it is prepared specially for ruminants; that is, animals which chew the cud.

Feed carrots, sliced, as often as you can get them. Horses also like swedes and turnips. These are fed whole; either thrown out into the field, or, with the stabled horse, one can be put into the manger at night.

Linseed must be cooked and simmered until the seeds are soft and the water glutinous before being made into a mash with bran, or fed as a gruel.

There are many vitamin and mineral supplements, or additives, on the market. Take your pick. Some of the best are those compounded of seaweed. Cod-liver oil is a good winter additive, but must be fed in small quantities, in only one feed per day.

For a horse in ordinary work, a reliable concentrate ration would be half the total ration consisting of cubes, and the remainder, a mixture of cereal: oats, barley or in winter, flaked maize; bran, and sugar beet when available. Even this may need to be varied according to the horse's work and temperament. If it seems to need a little more sparkle, give more oats and less, or no, cubes. If it is rather excitable, give more cubes, more sugar beet pulp and barley instead of oats. In fact, apart from giving it the right amount of food in weight, only experience can teach exactly how to feed each horse.

The hay ration should always be spaced out for the stabled horse or the horse brought in at night, so that it has the largest proportion at night. Night is a long time for a horse, which does not lie down and go to sleep for hours on end as we do. If it has finished its hay by nine o'clock and has nothing to do till seven the next morning, it will start eating its bed, or, through boredom, amuse itself by developing the irritating stable vices of crib-biting, wind-sucking, or weaving. It is a help if the horse has a salt or mineral lick in its box, or field, if out.

A horse should not be worked until it has had time to digest its concentrate feed. This will take from three-quarters of an hour to an hour. If it is worked on a full stomach, the stomach, being distended, will press on the lungs and cause discomfort in breathing. If a horse has had a long and hard day's work, it is better on returning to give it a bran mash, which is easily digested, than its normal concentrate feed. It can have its normal feed later in the evening.

It is essential to worm regularly, at least every three months.

Although it is obvious that it is cruel to underfeed horses, because they show their lack of feeding by looking poor and ribby, it is almost as cruel to overfeed them, especially small ponies, which can become so grossly overweight that they develop laminitis. This is an inflammation of the foot which is very painful, difficult to cure, and always liable to recur. For this reason, in spring and early summer, when the grass is rich and lush, ponies that normally live out should if possible be brought in for at least a part of every day. If this isn't possible, it is worth while getting an electric fence and letting them strip graze the field, eating one strip until it is really bare. If a horse has been in all winter, it is also wise to limit its grazing time when first turned out by day; this is *essential* if the grass is lush — otherwise colic or laminitis is very likely to occur. Any change of diet should be gradual.

In principle, it is correct that horses should drink before eating, but if they always have water available, they will never drink too much. Some seem to enjoy eating part of their feed, having a slosh round in the bucket, and back to the feed.

In very cold weather, horses and ponies wintering out, and getting their water from a trough, will have to have the ice broken for them. If there is running water in the field they can break any ice that may form with their hooves. This may not be possible in very cold regions of the USA.

General care

However much you may want to have your own horse, before you buy one it really is advisable to get some practical experience of horse care and stable management. You can learn how, and on what, to feed a horse from books. You can only learn how to handle one by actually doing it. Besides, when you started learning to ride, you may have had little, or no, previous experience of horses; you may even, although you liked them, have been a bit wary of them 'on the ground'; they are, after all, rather large, and strong! Before buying a horse, it really is important that you should have complete confidence in your ability to handle it. Go into its box and feed it; groom it, lift and pick out its feet without thinking it may kick you through the door, put on and take off its tack, lead it on a headcollar, and catch it in its field, and lead it in. The school where you are having lessons may be able to help you, by letting you stay on after rides, and work, and learn; or, you may have a horse-owning friend who'll be glad to let you help look after it.

You must also be sure that you can afford the money it will cost to keep it, and that you are always going to have the time to care for it properly. Horses are entirely and absolutely dependent on humans for everything — for their food, water, comfort, and maintenance of their health. To own a horse, therefore, while it will give you a lot of pleasure, also means, or should mean, that you are willing to accept the responsibility of caring for it; day in, day out; fine weather or foul!

Provided you have bought a horse you really like, you will find that caring for it gives you as much pleasure as riding. Also, as time goes on, you will find a mutual understanding developing between you and the horse, which will help your riding. You will feel you and the horse beginning to work together; to form a partnership.

As a great many people today have full- or part-time, jobs, it is probable you will keep your horse either on the combined system, or, if it is of suitable type, out. Obviously, you are going to have to arrange the horse's feeding times to fit in with your own daily routine. Once established, you must stick to those times as closely as possible. Horses are creatures of habit; they seem to have clocks in their stomachs.

A horse kept on the combined system is in at night and out by day in wnter; reversed, in summer. This means that in winter, one must get up early enough to feed the horse before breakfast. Then, before going to work, take it out to its field; New Zealand-rugged if necessary, and with a haynet if the ground is bare, or frost-hard. Be very careful when hanging a haynet to make sure it will not hang so low when empty that the horse might catch his leg in it. Its box should then be mucked out; either leaving it to air during the day, or setting the bed ready again for the evening. The water bucket should be removed before mucking out.

When brought in, the horse need not be groomed thoroughly,

but it must be brushed over and its feet picked out. If rugged, the rugs changed; a feed given, and a small net, or quantity, of hay. Considerably later, say between seven and nine, whatever time is most likely to be permanently convenient, it should be settled for the night. The water bucket must be refilled; a large night haynet given; and the rug checked for position. If it is the evening before the horse is to be ridden, it can have a third concentrate feed after the ride.

At weekends, while one will be riding, one may also want to have a 'lie in'. This cannot be explained to the horse. One can go back to bed afterwards, but it must have its first feed at the usual time or everyone's peace will be disturbed by neighings, door bangings and other equine distress signals.

On riding days, the horse will not be turned out and one can adopt normal stable routine: early feed and small haynet; then, before riding, mucking out: tie the horse up while doing this. As the horse will be standing in at least part of the day, lay a daybed. That is, bank up most of the re-usable straw round the sides of the box, leaving just a fair covering on the floor. Horses should not be left standing any length of time on a bare floor: they may want to stale — pass water — and will not do so if they are going to splash themselves.

Before riding the horse need only be brushed over, mane and tail tidied and feet picked out; thorough grooming can be left till later in the day. Grooming a horse thoroughly is an energetic process which should take at least three-quarters of an hour. If, in cold weather, one grooms in gloves, always finish by taking them off, and running the bare hands down the horse's legs, over the saddle patch and under the forearms. Bumps, scratches, unusual lumps or tender places can only be felt with the ungloved fingers. Grooming not only makes a horse look nice. It keeps the skin healthy and supple, the pores open, and if done energetically, the muscles toned up. If there is time, therefore, it will appreciate a thorough grooming even on non-riding days.

In summer, the horse on the combined system can stay out all the time when not being ridden, but it must be visited each morning and evening. If it is to keep fit, it is wiser to bring it in before going to work, give it a feed, water, and a net of hay and leave it in its box, bedded. This, however, is really only possible if there is someone about who can replenish the water and refill the haynet at midday. The advantage of doing this is that the horse is in, ready to be ridden in the light evenings; also, that when the grass is rich, it will not be eating it for twenty-four hours, and getting grossly over-fat.

Horses and ponies living out should not, in winter, be groomed thoroughly, even on riding days. Some grease must be left in their coats, for warmth and to keep the coats waterproof. But they must be kept clean; their legs free of mud, their feet regularly picked out and their manes and tails kept untangled. Always, winter and summer, after riding and before being turned out, the saddle patch and behind the elbows where the girth lies should be well brushed and freed of any caked and dried sweat. If a horse or pony living out comes in shivering with cold after a wet, windy night, it must be dried off and warmed. Take the worst of the wet off with a wisp of straw; then put a layer of clean straw over its back and throw a rug, or a clean sack if you have no rug, over the straw. Dry its *ears* with a stable rubber. And buy the animal a New Zealand rug; it is obviously too thin-skinned to winter out without one.

Any horse that comes in from a ride wet and sweaty, or just sweaty, can be dried off by 'thatching' it with straw, and then putting over the straw either an anti-sweat rug, or its night rug, *inside out*, so that the inside of the rug stays dry. And always dry its ears. The ears are good indicators of horse-warmth: cold, or cold and wet ears: cold horse; warm, even if wet, ears: warm horse.

No one should try to do their own horse-doctoring. But everyone who owns a horse should know a little about horse first aid, and know when a horse is in definite need of veterinary treatment.

A healthy horse should be alert; the eyes bright, the skin supple, the coat lying flat. The membranes of the eyes, and nostrils, should be a clear salmon pink. Its normal temperature is 100° F (37.7° C); and its pulse rate, at rest, between 36 and

40 beats per minute. The temperature is taken by inserting the thermometer, Vaselined, into the rectum. Any rise over 101° F (38·3° C), call the veterinary surgeon immediately. In the USA normal temperature varies between 100° F (37·7° C) and 101·5° F (38·6° C). It may rise slightly in the afternoon and of course, drastically after work). In the USA your vet will probably not feel it necessary to call him unless it is over 102° F (38·9° C).

If a horse is off its food, dull of eye, head hanging, coat 'staring': that is, harsh and standing out from the skin rather than lying flat, take its temperature, and call the vet, telling him the thermometer reading. Don't wait till next day, hopefully thinking the horse may be better by then.

If a horse is eating well, possibly even ravenously, and instead of putting on condition it has a pot-belly, it has worms. Give it a worm dose; there are many excellent ones on the market. Call the vet only if, after three weeks or so, it still fails to put on condition.

If the horse paws the ground, rolls, kicks at its stomach, probably sweats, it has colic. Call the vet at once. Keep the horse warm and keep it walking till the vet arrives.

If it has a runny nose, and possibly a cough, it may have just a cold, or it may be developing equine influenza. Call the vet. Nowadays, equine influenza is so prevalent that any horse going to shows, or coming into contact with strange horses, should have a yearly anti-influenza injection. All horses should be immunized against tetanus. Consult the vet about this.

If a horse goes lame on a ride, get off, and pick up its feet. The most obvious cause of lameness is often overlooked: a stone in the shoe. Remove the stone, and the horse will go sound. If there is no stone, lead the horse home and call the vet. Do not risk making the lameness worse by riding home.

If in the slightest doubt as to your horse's health, always call the vet; and always do exactly what he tells you. If a horse is lame, and he says rest it for six weeks, rest it for six. Don't start riding it again after four because it seems to be all right.

First aid for cuts and scratches is simple. Clean thoroughly, with tepid water and a very little mild disinfectant, Dettol or similar. In the USA the equivalent of Dettol is probably the disinfectant Betadine. Once clean, keep the wound dry, and leave to heal open to the air and dusted with antiseptic powder. With a pair of blunt-ended scissors, trim the hair away from the edges of the cut. Only call the vet if a cut appears to need stitching, and if the horse has not been immunized against tetanus. Puncture wounds, which can be made by thorns or barbed wire or really anything sharp and pointed, are more difficult to clean. A good way is to put on a kaolin poultice. When there is no longer any pus on the poultice cloth, the wound is clean. In the USA a veterinarian might recommend a Furazone sweat for a puncture wound instead of a kaolin poultice.

Against emergencies, keep, in the stable or tack room:

A bottle of mild disinfectant. A container of antiseptic dusting powder. A jar of zinc ointment. A large roll of cotton wool. A couple of crepe bandages. Some pieces of clean linen or cotton, for pads or for putting on poultices. A tin of kaolin poultice. A pair of sharp, blunt-ended scissors. At least two doses of worm medicine. Anything else will be added when, and if, necessary, by the veterinary surgeon.

A sick horse, like a sick person, appreciates care, and company. Although every horse owner hopes it will never happen, there may well come to all of us a time when only almost hourly care will bring about a sick horse's recovery. Not to give this, or to give it grudgingly, is not to have fully accepted the responsibility of owning, and caring for, a horse.

7 The mind of the horse

Different kinds of animals have different kinds of behaviour patterns: instinctive reactions, which have been conditioned by the ways in which they had to live, protect themselves, and find their food, when in the wild. On certain domesticated animals, the horse and dog in particular, man has been able to superimpose a new set of patterns. The better this is done, the better we say the horse or dog is trained. However, as we can never entirely eradicate the old ones, it is a help to have some idea of what they are: why they exist, and why sometimes the best trained horse or dog can revert to them. Horses and dogs, the two animals whose training concerns us most, are totally different kinds of animal. We all know that the horse is a 'herbivore': a grazing animal; and that the dog is a 'carnivore': a meat eater. But the difference goes deeper than that. The dog, like all carnivores, (ourselves included) is by nature a 'predator': a hunter. The horse, in the wild, is a hunted, or preyed upon, animal.

For this reason, the horse is by nature conditioned to being constantly on the alert for danger, to be suspicious of the unknown or the strange, and to take refuge in flight from what appears threatening. One stallion may fight another for possession of his mares; some mares will show fight to protect their foals. But in the wild, it is only the herd leader, the senior stallion or sometimes an elderly mare, which will stand and show fight to an outside enemy to protect the herd. The horse is not by nature aggressive. The dog, on the other hand, conditioned to preying on, and killing, other animals for its food, is naturally aggressive. However well-trained, it is perpared to fight for its rights if necessary; and will fight a threat rather than run.

The horse, like most herbivores, is gregarious: a herd animal. It feels safe within the protection offered by the discipline and protocol established and upheld by the herd leader. It is not suddenly, are annoying equine behaviour patterns, which the novice rider can find both alarming, and unsettling to seat and confidence. With the gradual acceptance of the unfamiliar that comes with training, these habits tend to disappear, although even the best trained horse can be startled into shying.

Shying is not something the horse does deliberately to annoy its rider. Its instinctive reaction is always to get away from anything that gives it a sudden fright. The reason the horse so often seems to us unreasonably startled, is largely due to the way it sees things, which is different from the way we see them. Our eyes are set fairly close together, frontally in our skulls. We have a wide range of bi-focal vision, but see little to either side, and nothing to the rear. The horse's eyes are set wide apart. Each eye can see a great deal to the side, and quite a lot to the rear, but its range of bi-focal vision, both eyes seeing the object at the same time, is very narrow. Something seen fleetingly with one eye is far less understandable than the same thing seen bi-focally: in the round, as it were. This is why we sometimes think our horses are shying 'at nothing': they have seen something to one side or the other, or behind them, which we cannot see. It also explains why a horse can pass something with no trouble in one direction, and shy at it when returning, in the opposite one. Unless it has been able to see the object bi-focally, it is seeing it each time with a different eye. When a horse wants really to inspect something new or strange, it always turns its head directly towards it, so as to get it into its line of bi-focal vision. The best way to prevent, or counteract, shying, is always to ride positively and confidently, communicating to the horse the feeling that so long as you are on top, in charge, it has nothing to fear. This doesn't mean you can never let your horse relax, riding on a long rein, 'on trust', as Henry Wynmalen (author of *Equitation*, the classic book on horsemanship) put it. It simply means you must keep your mind on what you, and the horse, are doing. If you ride along in a daze, it is your fault if your horse leaps to the side when your dog comes out of the bushes, and puts you down! You knew the dog was there, you shouldn't have let the horse forget.

Whether or not horses see colour is debatable. While it seems to be generally agreed that they do not see colour in the same way we do, they can certainly differentiate between light and dark colours, and varying colour densities. Nearly all horses react differently at first to jumps made of brightly coloured, shiny, painted poles, than to those made of natural-coloured wood, or greenery. Probably this is because the different shiny colours appear as degrees of colour brightness and density not seen in nature, and so are, correctly, taken to be 'unnatural' and most animals, ourselves included, are wary of the 'unnatural'.

Horses have a keen sense of smell, and rely on it more than we realize. While they also have acute hearing and recognize people by their voices, rather than by their looks, smell must also play a part in recognition. They cannot tell men from women by their clothes — nor can we always, for that matter; nor necessarily by their voices. There must be, to them, a difference of smell, fortunately undetectable by ourselves! How otherwise does a horse which has been mishandled or ill-treated by a man, or a woman, retain a suspicion of one sex or the other, and seem able to sense immediately which is which?

The horse's congenital dislike, and fear, of pigs is probably racial memory; the wild boar was an enemy of the wild horse. Horses get over this racial behaviour pattern if they live near domestic pigs, but practically every horse has the same instinctive initial reaction.

Considering that horses in the wild were conditioned to living constantly on the alert, ready to run from any threat to their freedom, it is surely one of man's greatest achievements that he has been able to dominate, and impose entirely new behaviour patterns, on these highly sensitive animals. By obtaining their confidence, and giving them security, he has transmuted their free power and energy into the courage, speed, obedience and controlled strength of the domesticated horse. If that confidence is not to be abused, or undermined. it is necessary to be aware of the many instincts which a young horse has to overcome in the course of training, and to which, in moments of stress or panic, even the trained horse can revert.

Glossary of US equivalents

Britain	USA	Britain	USA
bandages	leg wraps	numnah	saddle pad
broken wind	heaves	over at the knee	calf kneed
cracked heel	scratches; greased heel	overreach boots	bell boots
		paddock	corral
cubes	pellets	rasp teeth or hooves	float teeth or hooves
field	paddock		
fortnight	two weeks	remove shoes	reset shoes
girth	cinch; girth	rise to the trot	post
good doer	good keeper	rosette	ribbons
hacking; riding out	pleasure or trail riding	rug, rugging	blanket, blanketing
halter	rope halter	sack	feed bag
headcollar	halter	society; organization	conference
horse box	van		
laminitis	founder	stable rubber	stable towel
loose box	box stall	stirrup treads	stirrup pads
lorry	truck	tarred road	black top
maize	corn	travel a horse	truck a horse

Useful addresses

Britain

The British Horse Society; The Pony Club, British Equestrian Centre, Kenilworth, Warwickshire CV8 2LR

Ponies of Britain Club, MRS GLENDA SPOONER, Brookside Farm, Ascot, Berkshire

The Association of British Riding Schools, Chesham House, 56 Green End Road, Sawtry, Cambridgeshire

The BHS and ABRS issue lists of approved riding schools; the POBC, a list of approved riding holiday establishments.

USA

American Horse Council, 1700 K Street NW, Washington, DC 20006

Pleasure Horse Club, Box 6, Dana Point, California 92629

United States Pony Clubs, 303 South High Street, West Chester, Pennsylvania 19380